I'm a Stranger Here Myself

by John Seymour

THE FAT OF THE LAND
THE COMPLETE BOOK OF SELF-SUFFICIENCY
THE COUNTRYSIDE EXPLAINED

by John and Sally Seymour

SELF-SUFFICIENCY
*The Science and Art of Producing and Preserving
your own Food*

I'm a Stranger Here Myself

The Story of a Welsh Farm

JOHN SEYMOUR

FABER AND FABER
London & Boston

First published in 1978
by Faber and Faber Limited
3 Queen Square London WC1N 3AU
Printed in Great Britain by
Latimer Trend & Company Ltd Plymouth
All rights reserved

© *1978 John Seymour*

British Library Cataloguing in Publication Data

Seymour, John, b. 1914
   I'm a stranger here myself.
   1. Family farms—Wales—Newport
(District)
   I. Title
   640   S458.5.N/

ISBN 0-571-11234-X

Contents

Contents

1   *In the Belly of the Whale*

With a creaking of rusty springs the heavy, iron-bound wooden door of the Whale swung down towards the ground and I found myself gazing into the vast interior.

'It's enormous,' said Sally, my wife.

'It'd make a good house,' said Jane, our ten-year-old eldest daughter.

'We could drive the Fish Van right up inside it and carry it that way,' said Ann, who was seven. Kate, five, didn't say anything very enlightening, and Dai, our son, didn't say anything at all because he hadn't been born yet.

In the Punjab, it is said that if a man owns a piece of Earth he owns a piece of Heaven; for by law he owns the space above the Earth and this space must, indeed, extend upwards all the way to Paradise. I don't know how sound this is theologically, legally, or astronomically; but I do know that Sally and I had long wished to own a piece of Earth, if not of Heaven, and were tired of only being able to rent five acres of both. Surely every denizen of this Earth is entitled to a piece of it? But with the price of Earth driven Heavenward in Suffolk by City gentlemen wishing to shoot pheasants, we were forced to seek abroad.

Abroad for us, in the event, meant Pembrokeshire. Having spent most of my life travelling in such countries as Damaraland, Ethiopia, Barotseland and Sri Lanka, I had never had time to go to Wales, and this was *terra incognita* to me. At the age of four, Sally had once gone to Capel y Ffin with her mother and father to visit their friend Eric Gill, and had been stung by a bee. That was all she could remember of her visit to the Principality. But we had been invited over by smallholding friends and had instantly fallen in love with the country—a love not in any way tempered by finding out that good agricultural land there could be bought for sixty pounds an acre and that there were practically no pheasants.

Here was a country that belonged to the countryman! This was a smiling sunny country of hills of a humane size, splendid wooded valleys, sweeping fertile uplands and a coastline that would make any coast in the Mediterranean look dowdy. And I had imagined Wales to be a land of gloomy mountains and wet sheep.

So after getting back from our visit to our friends, I had returned to Pembrokeshire in the Fish Van (we called it the Fish Van because it was a fish van) and had bought a farm. Seventy-two acres of land, perhaps forty of them any good, a house that had been empty for more than a year and pretty neglected for many years before that (it had been a *tenanted* farm—and what tenant is going to look after his landlord's house with the love and devotion with which he would look after his own?), some ruinous farm buildings, one iron gate across the drive and not one other gate, nor one yard of fence, nor one yard of ditch or drain anywhere else on the farm.

I bought this place for £4250, which meant about £4500 by the time I had paid commissions and all the rest of it.

I did not *have* £4500. In fact it would be an understatement to say that I did not have a farthing—for I had an overdraft of £250 at the bank and absolutely no security. But I went to the agent and just bought the farm. Buy first and worry about it later was my policy. And if you act in this way, I have always found, somebody—some Thing or some Power (or maybe just yourself?)—always manages to pull your chestnuts out of the fire. In this case the vendor, a local squire who was busy selling off his estate, gave me a mortgage at six per cent for half the sum and my bank manager, Mr. Birkinshaw of the Midland Bank, Oxford Circus, let me increase my overdraft for the other half. In addition to this Sally had been presented with a house in Mallorca by her mother. This house we were trying to sell, and eventually did for £1500, but it took a year to get the money, and by that time we had squandered far more on premature and ill-considered draining operations. So we did not buy Fachongle Isaf, our farm, with nothing. We bought it with considerably *less* than nothing.

And having bought it, we had the small problem of getting ourselves and all our animals, goods and chattels over to it.

And this, we realized, was a much more difficult problem than merely buying a farm.

The Fish Van was, like most fish vans, a seven-hundredweight Ford. We couldn't carry much in that. We had a horse and governess cart, three cows, a flock of geese, another of ducks, two dogs, a herd of cats, another of children (three small girls), a charming eighteen-year-old girl named Sheila who worked for us (Sally is a potter, and was always able to pay a girl—whom I called the Handmaiden—out of her earnings), a flock of hens, another of cockerels, twenty or thirty pigs, and then a vast store of what auctioneers call 'dead stock': hundreds of split chestnut fencing posts, old corrugated iron sheets including 'Anderson Shelter' sections—those heavy curved sheets so useful to the pig farmer but so difficult to pack—pig houses, hen arks, a whole junk-yard-full of horse-drawn implements (for we were still living—as we are partially now—in the horse-transport age), chick brooders, rolls and rolls of barbed wire and wire netting, electric fences, iron standards, hundreds of tools, and a houseful of furniture. Thousands of items in fact, each one of which would fetch practically nothing if we tried to sell it but which would make us reach deep into our purse if we tried to replace it. What did something like an almost-new bow saw go for in a sale in those days, some thirteen years ago? Half a crown? But it was thirty bob if you tried to buy a new one. That was about the rate of exchange.

As for the animals—well, many of them were part of the family and we could no more leave them behind than we could our children. Almost—I suppose if we had had to make a choice . . . The pigs we did sell—we thought we could pick them up cheaper in Wales.

As we thought about it our new home began to seem as inaccessible to us as the Moon. It would have taken the biggest pantechnicon available three journeys to get that lot across—and would have cost us, we found, six hundred pounds. Worse still, we would have had no time to load. To load so many items of such diversity we knew would take days. The hired pantechnicon would be charging us so much for every hour that it waited. And why did we, who had been living the Simple Life for eight years at this little smallholding in Suffolk, require this immense collection of knick-knacks? Because that is what you have to have if you lead the Simple Life—just read what Robinson Crusoe found he had to have on his island.

We even thought of *walking* the stock over and driving in the horse and cart. We certainly never considered this in the case of the pigs of course, as anybody who has ever tried driving a pig more than a few yards will understand. I have always thought that the swineherds who are mentioned in the Bible were people who went where the pigs wanted to go—not the other way round. Goose-girls were better off; geese can be driven easily enough. As for cattle and sheep—I have driven these (helped by African herdsmen, I should add) many hundreds of miles in Africa and they will actually put on weight, and fatten, during the journey. But Africa is one place and the A40 just outside Gloucester during the rush-hour is another. Wage-earners stream in thousands from those vast concrete factories where they make—what? Gloucester Gladiators?—and executives in puce-coloured cars join them; a score of tributary roads bring their separate floods to join the main, stinking, slowly crawling glacier of traffic; Sally is driving the governess cart; the kids and I run behind chasing cows (one of which is just about to calve)—hens—cocks—geese—ducks—no! No, no! Get to our new home we would somehow or other. But not like that. Three hundred and forty-five miles—from the most easterly tip of England to the most westerly (nearly) tip of Wales.

So we began to search for a cattle lorry. If we could buy a farm with a minus quantity of money, we argued, so we could a cattle lorry. We saw cattle lorries large, small and simply colossal. Of course when you want to *buy* a cattle lorry they are like gold—everybody wants them. When we came to *sell* ours —well, that was another story. But in the end we found one, seven tons burthen though she would carry many times that weight, diesel-engined, and simply enormous. It seemed to take quite a long time to walk from one end of her to the other. We bought her from a horse-dealer for five hundred and fifty pounds of Mr. Birkinshaw's money.

'So you want to buy a cattle lorry?' the latter said resignedly, when I telephoned him.

'Yes.'

'Well, I suppose nothing will stop you?'

'No.'

'All right then—buy the cattle lorry,' he sighed.

We bought her late in the evening, and I climbed up into the driver's seat trying to look as if I was used to climbing up into drivers' seats several yards above the ground. I also tried to look as if I knew how to start the thing. The nice young horse-dealer who had sold her to us showed me how, the powerful diesel engine roared into life (and I mean roared—I was to suffer that roaring for many hours during the following weeks) and I gingerly put her into gear. She rolled forward. Sally followed me in the Fish Van.

I stalled her when I came to the end of the farm drive. When I swung on to the public highway I was alarmed to find that she needed a lot of land to turn in. Fortunately the tree I drove over was a fairly small one. I was then disturbed to discover that she appeared to fill the small country road as a piston fills a cylinder. I would simply pump all lesser traffic before me. But when a car appeared, and I pulled over until I scraped the trees, the car—looking to me like a tiny black beetle down below—passed by quite safely. I began to feel the confidence that comes with size. I would be able, I realized, to press on regardless, and smaller fry would give me a wide berth. I would just pretend they weren't there.

I seemed to be thundering through the night at a tremendous speed, but afterwards Sally told me I never actually hit thirty, although I came very close to it several times, and that an ever-growing convoy of furious drivers steamed along behind me like the tail of a comet. Well, I said, that would teach them the habit of patience.

Next morning, after we had milked the cow and fed the live-stock and ourselves, we started to load the Whale, as we had named our new vehicle.

First the heaviest thing of all—the Cambridge roller. This is a roller formed of ridged rings. Ours is pulled by a horse, and what it weighs I don't know, but if a Cambridge roller goes over your toe you know it is heavy, and particularly when you have to drag it up a ramp. However, with the aid of block-and-tackle and much ingenuity, we hauled it into the Whale and firmly lashed it down. Then in went a hay-rake, several ploughs, cultivators, harrows, seed-drills, horse-hoes, pig troughs, iron sheeting, fencing posts; bulky and heavy odds and ends of every description. Sally is a marvel at packing things and we worked so that hardly a cubic inch was wasted. We took a week over it —bartering time for *space*. If we had hired a van, and had had to load it in a day, we would have been obliged to content ourselves with half the load.

And at 3 a.m., on Sunday the 28th of March, Sally and I climbed up into the high cab of the Whale and alarmed the pigeons in the nearby pine wood by starting the engine.

We were sure we were grossly overloaded but there was no possible way of confirming this. We opened, and then shut, the two gates on the sandy track that separated our old home, the Broom, from the rest of the world, and soon we were driving along the deserted roads of East Anglia in fine style.

We bowled along one road—only to remember in the nick of time that there was a low railway bridge over it. I had been under this a hundred times in lesser vehicles and out of habit might easily have slammed on through, either taking the bridge with us or leaving the upper half of the Whale behind. We managed to turn, and went another way, having learned one important lesson for Whale-drivers.

By the time day broke we had reached the M1 at Newport Pagnell. We didn't go on the motorway but parked the Whale on a side-road and surreptitiously sneaked up a service road for breakfast in the motorway café. After this we drove continuously, except for a break at midday for a pint of beer and a pork pie, and another at four o'clock for the cup of tea which no true-born Englishman can ever do without, and we got to our new farm at half-past six in the afternoon—fifteen and a half hours after we had started.

We were whacked. It had been hard work driving the Whale. The roar from the engine was deafening. As the day advanced the roads had filled up with holiday traffic—little tin boxes crawling through the hills of Wales and not letting us pass them. *They* were not in a hurry—we were. Sometimes we had to grind along for miles in second gear. The effort of swinging the Whale round corners made me sweat. I began to find a new sympathy for lorry drivers. They have a hard, nerve-wracking and un-healthy job. The provision of power-assisted steering for them, well-meant as it no doubt is, only makes the job worse—for it takes the physical effort out of it, and it is that physical effort that keeps a man at least partially fit (even though he may live almost entirely on white bread and fried food).

It took us an hour, with Sally shouting and me steering, to back the enormous Whale into the incredibly difficult, narrow and steeply down-hill drive. I realized that if I went down head-first I would never get her out again. We dropped the ramp and pulled out some camping gear, lit a fire in the open yard and cooked a good meal on it. Mutton chops, onions and potatoes and good wholemeal bread—all (except the wheat for the bread) grown on our little homestead in Suffolk. Would we be able to do as well for ourselves in this new, strange, very foreign land?

We walked round the farm a little and chased off hundreds of strange sheep and scores of cattle. Being completely unfenced the place was full of neighbours' stock. We had not yet explored our property. We began to find, once away from the semi-ruinous buildings, that the farm was pretty much in the same state. To the north of the house was a very steep hill behind which lay four good fields—the best on the farm. They were separated one from another by low stone-and-earth banks (locally called 'hedges') with sparse thorn and elder hedges on them, which could have served no purpose in keeping any stock either in or out. Beyond the four good fields was a hinterland of marsh and scrub. If you went down a very soggy green lane to the west of the house you came to wet woodland of an im-penetrability to compare with the Burma jungle. If you turned left off the lane short of the woods you came to eight acres of swamp in which you could lose a herd of water buffalo. South, and very difficult of access, were four tiny fields which were well-drained but full of rocks; below them, to the west, four narrow fields which seemed quite clean and good—very good land in fact, but tiny.

The farm was terribly rough—much of it, in fact, sheer wilderness. It was nice to know that, in these crowded islands, such wilderness still existed. But it was beautiful. The little fields were surrounded and screened by sessile oaks—not straight towering trees but pretty stunted and crooked ones—big ash, holly and alder. Each of the fields other than the four behind the steep hill seemed like clearings in a great forest.

One thing we would never go short of was water. No less than three little streams ran past the house, and the west frontier of the farm was a small river: the Clydach. The farmhouse itself seemed to have been sited on a line of springs: at the foot of a small mountain which collected the rains of heaven and debouched them into plain air—at one point actually in our back kitchen. The mountain was crowned with some great rock cairns called Carnau Meibion Owen—the Cairns of the Sons of Owen —which interested me, my mother being of the Owen family, albeit the Maryland branch. I assumed that the man who had chosen this site to build a house on must have been semi-aquatic. It was obvious that the farm had been laboriously drained in the distant past; there were artificial stream-beds on it, and the remains of ditches long silted up were just discernible. I had the impression that this was a land that had once been well and carefully farmed, but had been neglected for at least half a century.

From every point of the farm you could see one thing: the top of another rugged, rocky, romantic little mountain, which I later found was called Carn Ingli. This has been dubiously translated by most people as 'the Carn of the Angels', but Ingli just does not mean angels in the Welsh language, nor ever did. 'Angels' it *should* mean though—for a more fitting place for angels to congregate than the top of that little mountain could not be found. It lay to the west of us—we live in its evening shadow and for twelve years now it has never left our consciousness. Somehow I find it very hard to imagine a life without Carn Ingli rising like a rocky rampart in the West.

We dragged a mattress out of the Whale, flung it on the concrete floor of the living-room of the little house, and went to bed. Because the windows were all nailed shut—and obviously had been for years—we left the door open.

I awoke in the night feeling that Something was in the room. There was a sound of heavy breathing, and it was not my wife. Something huge moved over me. I could feel hot breath. I knew

16

the smell of that breath—it was sweet breath, smelling of clover and grass.

'Go away,' I said. There was a loud plopping noise as a bullock made for the door leaving a copious offering of bullock dung behind. 'Our neighbours are going to resent us!' I said to Sally, who had woken in some alarm. 'They're losing some valuable free grazing.'

We spent three days unloading the Whale, for we carefully stowed everything where it would have to go, in the ruinous buildings. This was to save days of labour when we really moved in several months later. I had always lived in the country and assumed that things unlocked would just not get stolen and I was right. The man who invented the nursery rhyme that begins 'Taffy was a Welshman . . .' couldn't have known the Taffies round our way. In twelve years I don't think we have lost a thing.

We tried to buy a return cargo: cattle, sheep, donkeys—anything. We thought we might take a load of donkeys home to sell to the American airmen for their donkey-derbies—but when we found that they were fetching twenty pounds each in *Ireland* we gave up. After making exhaustive enquiries—mostly on the telephone from the nearest telephone box, which is a wretched way to do business—and after we had been told in a miserable voice by one lugubrious cattle-dealer that 'the bottom had dropped out of barren cows'—we decided to go back in ballast, or light. This was sad, for we had been hoping to recoup some of our expenses by taking a return load home. We were not *licensed* for carrying other people's stock, of course, but we could have bought cheap and sold dear. However, the merchant-adventurer cannot flourish in a world full of licences and permits to do this and that.

We left for our old home in the evening and drove through the night. Right through the City of London we drove—directly past St. Paul's—and we found that, provided we hit the City in the early hours of the morning, this was the best route. We made a second voyage with another huge load of dead stock. Then came the third, and last load, and that was the most difficult of all.

We loaded the front half of the Whale with furniture, cooking utensils, clothes, luggage, and all the rest of it. We had to clear and clean up as we went, for this was the final voyage. We were leaving the Broom for ever. Only the fact that we were too busy stowing things to stop and think for a *second* prevented it from being a very sad occasion.

The last night we all slept at the house of our very kind and forgiving landlord and his wife, Michael and Virginia Watson. This had an edge of sadness about it, for our children loved their children and we and they had grown used to each other in a tolerant sort of fashion, Michael even enduring Esau, our insatiable lurcher dog, who used to chase (and kill) his hares and in so doing play hell with his pheasants. Many a time Michael had driven up in his Landrover, accompanied by Backhouse his gamekeeper, with Esau firmly tied to a piece of string and looking very ashamed of himself (for being caught—*not* for poaching), and Michael—more in pain than in anger—saying 'Look John—really, you know—something will just have to happen, you know. . . . I really will have to take some action, you know . . .' And Esau had paid most faithful court to Michael's mother's little bitch, every time that animal had come on heat, keeping up a sad barking and howling far into the night just below her window. And yet, now that Esau was going, Michael seemed quite sad.

'I shall miss him, you know. Sort of got used to him.'

That last load was fearfully complicated. In every nook and cranny among the inanimate objects went the animate ones. The cats were locked up in the meat safe, over their heads went the geese—we actually stowed one goose sitting on a clutch of eggs! We made a nest for her, placed her carefully on her eggs, and shut her in with—objects. A forlorn hope, we knew, but it is blasphemous to destroy life except for a good purpose (to create or to sustain higher life). We had to *try* to save the little goose-lives inside the eggs. The hens were incarcerated somewhere far up inside the belly of the Whale, with beds, tables and chests of drawers all around them. There was a pottery kiln weighing at least half a ton somewhere in there, and an Aga cooker. The ducks were high up above everything else—they could see the world through the high ventilation slit. We erected a barricade across the Whale and drove in—or rather *pushed* in our three

18

cows. One of them, Miranda, a little Jersey, positively refused to go in. She had been on loan to Virginia, and Virginia dearly wanted to buy her. How foolish we were not to sell her! How mean and grasping and foolish. But it was as though she knew she was going to her death—although she was the gentlest of creatures she fought not to go in and we had practically to lift her bodily.

Another crazy barricade—and in went Bessie the mare. A big, and very old cart-horse of uncertain breed. Then up went the great ramp-door and its heavy bolts were banged home. Well, I thought, whatever they may do inside there, at least they are not going to get out.

It was eight o'clock in the evening when we slammed the door and we had been working flat out since early morning. Sally got in the Fish Van, with the dogs and children. Sheila climbed up with me. We said goodbye to our kind friends and thundered off into the night.

We were banking on coffee at all-night cafés. But we banked in vain. We did not know that these places close down on Saturday night. We did stop once though—to refuel. At three in the morning we drew up at a filling station and the sleepy attendant came reluctantly out of his cabin to fill our tank with diesel. Awakened by the sudden cessation of movement, all—but all— of the disparate birds and animals in the belly of the Whale gave tongue. The noise was deafening. The horse whinnied, the cows mooed, the cats yowled, the hens clucked, the geese hissed and the ducks—well, the ducks shoved their heads out of the ventilation-slot high up above the petrol attendant's head and quacked like fury.

'My Gawd,' he said, 'My Gawd—what's this? A flipping Noah's Ark?'

2   *Drop-ins and Other Matters*

No flopping down in the sun for a rest after the long drive as we had done before *that* time. No sooner had we made the difficult and arduous manoeuvre of backing down the drive than the ramp had to come down and we had to get those animals out of there at *any* price.

And what chaos was inside the belly of the Whale!

The horse had kicked down the barrier between her and the cows. The big animals were all mixed up together. The yowling of the cats in the meat safe was horrible. The goose eggs were broken and had dripped through the gauze onto the imprisoned cats. We opened the door of the meat safe and three furious felines—dripping with egg-yolk and goose-shit—streaked away into the undergrowth. 'That's the last of *them*,' I thought. The horse lit off in one direction, the cows in another; the geese went hissing off into the marshes, the ducks took wing, as far as they could; the hens and the cockerels flapped away into the trees. I then began to realize what a wonderful invention was the *fence*. There was no fence between us and London—between us and John O'Groats. We rounded things up as best we could—tried to urge everything to run away but to run away down into the marshes in the middle of the farm.

Only then was I able to light a fire and boil a kettle and make what I had been craving all night—a cup of coffee.

After this came a strenuous day of breaking-out fencing-wire, and stakes, and tools, and staples, and erecting somewhere to confine the ducks, and somewhere for the hens, and some paddock in which we could enclose the four-footed animals during the night. It was when I was engaged in the latter activity that I made my first real contact with one of our neighbours. A spare, aquiline, rather handsome old man whose name, I discovered later, was George Hughes, came up the road as I was straining some barbed wire along it.

'Hullo,' he said, in an accent so very strange to me. 'Are you the Englishman?'

I told him I was.

'She is a good mist-tress,' he said. I realized he was talking about the barbed wire. 'They don't like that one!' he said, and moved on. It took me a minute or two to work out what he meant. I was used to the East Anglian countryman's idiom. This was something quite new—a new way of looking at things. Of course he meant that barbed wire was a good mistress—i.e. could *control* things—barbed wire was probably feminine in his language. 'They' meant the animals. When George came back from wherever he had been, with his three sheep dogs at his heel, he said: 'Don't kill yourself don't kill yourself—do like I do—take things as they come!' I didn't take his advice, being a man of a different race and very foolish.

The perceptive reader will by now have said: 'Why didn't the fool get fences up and pens and things ready on his previous voyages, so that they were ready when the animals arrived?'

Well, it wasn't like that. I knew perfectly well *in theory* that that was the way to do it but I wasn't doing it in theory. I was actually having to do it and that was the way it worked out. Anyway, we didn't *lose* any animals, so who's grumbling? We did in fact lose the mare on the second day, but we found her with some other horses five miles away.

From the 12th of May to the 21st of June there is but one entry in my diary and it says *Obstacle race!* There are no further entries because I had neither time nor energy to make them, and it says *Obstacle race!* because life felt like that—just like an obstacle race!

I remember vividly one particular course of the race: laying on water to different parts of the house. There was an existing alkathene pipe which came from high up on the hillside—on George Hughes's land. The arrangement often is in Wales that each farmer draws his water through an alkathene pipe from a spring on the land of the neighbour who is above him on the mountainside: thus I draw mine from George Hughes and the farm below me draws its from my land.

But Fachongle Isaf had but one tap. [Incidentally, Fachongle Isaf is pronounced, in the North Pembrokeshire dialect, 'vachonglay eesha' and, in received Welsh, 'vachonglay essaf': *fach* means small; *ongle* may be a corruption of *ongl*—a corner; *isaf* means low. George Hughes lives in Fachongle Ganol—middle Fachongle. Fachongle Uchaf (upper Fachongle) is now unfortunately a holiday cottage.] Now we sybaritic Easterners wanted more than one tap—we wanted, for example, a bathroom, a lavatory, a hot water system, a tap in the garden. I suppose we were marvellously lucky, really, to have a tap at all. The denizens of Fachongle Isaf had survived, and survived very well without one for no doubt hundreds, if not thousands, of years. There was, and is, a superb little spring a hundred yards from the house, in which a jet of clear water bubbles incessantly out of clean sand and spreads out to run down a wide shallow watercress bed. The denizens would have carried this water in wooden buckets, possibly slung from a yoke, and would have done their laundering in a stream (there is one a few yards from the house) and life would have been very pleasant for them.

Anyway, without going on about it, we definitely needed more than one tap. I had done plumbing with galvanized steel piping, mostly in South West Africa or what is now called Namibia. I had never worked with alkathene. The latter, of course, is supposed to be much easier, but like all the products of advanced technology it is only easy if you have *all* the parts. You can improvise nothing. With technology as advanced as steel piping you can cut pipe, thread it, bend it, join it. The old plumbers (and the very word came from lead) could *wipe* joints—join two pipes together by wiping molten lead about them. It took me a long time to find out that the alkathene pipe that led from the mountain was of an old alkathene that has to be held in boiling water before you can put a fitting on it, and that the fittings had to be slightly different from those currently in use, and that I had to have a complicated arrangement of different ones to match the old to the new—and . . . it feels like being in an obstacle race even to write about it all. No matter *how* many fittings I bought at the nearest builder's merchants (in Cardigan, ten miles away) there was always *one* fiddling little brass object that I did not have and could not do without.

But I think the most bizarre obstacle in the obstacle race was the ducks.

There was no back door to Fachongle Isaf. To get from the back of the house to the front you had to go right round it. Now the various pressures and urgencies on me at that time were such that I did everything at the double. I was like a man in an army 'glasshouse' or detention barracks. I could never allow myself to break into a walk. There just wasn't time. So in the course of this plumbing campaign I had to run between the back of the house and the front of the house perhaps a hundred times. The plumber always forgets his tools. I always forgot mine. They were always the wrong side of the house. And here we come to the ducks. We had a flock of twelve—white ones— and they had settled down to a happy life surrounding the house. Nothing would make them leave it. They only forebore to come inside because we kept the door shut. Now every time I had to leap from whatever I was doing, in this endless job of synthetic plumbing, to rush round the back to turn the water off at the main again—or on—or fetch a spanner, or whatever, I ran straight into a quacking, flapping mob of ducks. They would flee squawking before me; I would find it hard to break through them without actually treading on them; then when I came back again, again at the double, there they would be again, quacking deafeningly, until I came to believe that the lowest cell in Hell, reserved for property speculators or writers of snob-thrillers— was manned by ducks not devils—or devils in the form of ducks.

The house was in such a mess, and the weather was so fine, that for the first two months of our life there we cooked, like Gypsies, on a *yog*, or open fire in the yard. God knows there was enough firewood. The woods came almost right up to the house.

Of course besides plumbing there were several other little things to do. I remember the first time I entered the house, after it was ours, I made a savage attack on the linoleum. I cannot say I like linoleum—it seems to me to be one of the tattier products of our civilization—and here were *five layers* of it, one on top of the other, each with a more hideous pattern than the one underneath. Of course, when it rained, water bubbled out of the floor of the *gegin fach*—the small kitchen—ran through the

23

door that led to the living-room, carrying matchsticks and fag ends with it on into the flood, and disappeared under the linoleum. I suppose our predecessors had laid down layer after layer of the filthy stuff in an effort if not to stop, at least to hide this flood.

Then there was the wallpaper. Layers and layers of hideous wallpaper. Ripped down it all had to be, to disclose well-built stone walls.

A revealing thing was said by one of our neighbours, months later when we began to know a few of them, about the attitude behind this lino-laying activity. He was remarking on the fact that I was laying a slate floor.

'There's strange,' he said. 'We people are fighting to put all that old stuff behind us. We were brought up with rough things and we're trying to get away from all that—stone floors, stone walls. We like modern things—plastic, formica, electric cooking. we hate bare stone houses. We want them plastered—better still, built of brick or concrete blocks and then plastered. But you English people coming here—you seem to be the other way. You rip out lino and wallpaper and have bare stone walls. You lay old rough slate floors. There's strange.'

There's natural too, perhaps. And maybe the people who were brought up in 'rough surroundings', and who have achieved their ambition of living in something like a Hollywood film star's home, will give rise to a generation which will value the look of natural material again: stone, wood, straw, reeds, tiles—simple things near to the earth. Why, I see signs already. Didn't I see, the other day, a room on a neighbouring farm in which the natural stone walls had been plastered, and hung with wall-paper—wallpaper made to look like natural stone! There's progress!

Well, we ripped our lino out, layer after layer of it, and made a great stinking bonfire of it, rendered a thousand earwigs and woodlice homeless, and allowed the flood waters to run happily in the open instead of secretly under linoleum. We found a good slate floor beneath it all. That was in the living-room. In the other—the drawing-room—that sacred room that had probably been reserved since it was built for entertaining the Baptist Minister—we uncovered concrete. But we heard of a farmer some miles away who was scrapping an old cowshed to build a modern milking bale and who would sell us, for not very much, the slate slabs from it. We drove there in the Whale, loaded a ton or two of huge slate slabs, drove them back and laid them, in the drawing-room, on a layer of clean sand. It was just like a giant jigsaw puzzle, with each piece weighing a hundredweight or two. Foolishly, we bashed down the intervening wall between the two rooms. One word of advice to new settlers in strange lands. If you move into an existing house wait long and think hard before you alter it. There may be a reason for things being as they are. What we didn't know, but were to discover, was that the fire in one room fought against the fire in the other; each one competing for the air in the room and the stronger pulling the smoke down the weaker. At this time of writing the wall is back again, not the good solid wall of timber-framing and slate infill but a flimsy wall of fibre-board.

But now I realize that I have said no word so far of *why* we were leaving one remote smallholding, in the far east of Suffolk, to settle in another, in the far west of Wales. Were we farmers? Market gardeners? A twentieth-century Swiss Family Robinson? Well, perhaps the latter would be nearest to it. We were in those days, I believe, very rare birds. *Now* we are as common as people named Smith in London or cow farmers in Cardiganshire. We were neo-peasants, the New Homesteaders. Up till then I knew of nobody in the British Isles like us, although I had heard, through an American organization called the Green Revolution, that there were a growing number of us in America.

We were people who were consciously trying to break away from industry-dominated society and form a new kind of society—a simpler, less materialistic, less polluting, less dangerous kind, in close touch with the soil. We didn't know how to set about doing this—we don't now—but it seemed—and seems— to us self-sufficiency freaks that the *first* thing to do was to grow our own food.

So long as we were dependent for our very food on The Thing, as Cobbett called the unholy alliance between big industry and big government, then we were slaves to it body and soul. Cobbett, author of *Rural Rides, Cottage Economy*, and numerous other writings of the early nineteenth century, and described as 'the greatest living master of English prose' by the judge who sentenced him to prison once for high treason (he had attacked in his writings the flogging of some German mercenaries in the British Army) anticipated our own age's disquiet about uncontrolled industrial growth by a hundred and seventy years. He was the first writer to see that the growth, then in its infancy, of human institutions of an inhuman scale, was wrong and would lead to unhappiness, and he named the alliance between government, high finance and the rising big industry: *The Thing*. The Thing, he believed, was sucking the life and vigour out of the countryside, which is where he considered Man rightly belonged.

The so-called drop-out, or freak, or hippy, whether he lives in a pad in London or a broken-down cottage in the country, who depends on The Thing for his *food*, hasn't even started to drop out of anything. In any case, now that there are more and more of us self-sufficiency addicts, I think it is time we stopped using the term 'drop-out' and substituted for it the term 'drop-in'. A man who comes and joins us is dropping in to a sounder and more satisfying way of life and the thing he is dropping out of is falling to pieces anyway. So I call us *drop-ins*. A man living on national assistance, or 'the Health', or 'the Unemployment', or a man working for some huge organization which is itself part of The Thing, or living on money that Daddy supplies him with and which Daddy had earned from The Thing, is as much a part of it as the Prime Minister or the chairman of I.C.I. . . . He can grow the scruffiest beard in the world, wear his hair like a Comanche brave, puff pot until it makes him dizzy—but he is still right there slap in the middle of The Thing that he purports to hate and to be trying to get away from.

When he gets round to producing at least most of his own food—then at least he has started along the road that frees him from Cobbett's Thing. And then—the further step that we are all trying to make but really don't yet quite know how to— when he becomes part of a well-integrated organic community that produces most of its material needs from members' work, so as to become independent for *most* of its artifacts and materials —then he really is getting somewhere. A very good friend, who thinks the whole self-sufficiency movement silly, said to me: 'I'll take you seriously when you know how to make iron.'

Well, I *do* know how to make iron, and would make it if I wanted to, but it will be many centuries—nay, millennia—before the people of the new order use up all the iron that has already been made for silly and frivolous purposes. As George Bottomley wrote, in that splendid poem 'To Iron Founders and Others':

> When the old hollowed earth is cracked,
>   And when, to grasp more power and feasts,
> Its ores are emptied, wasted, lacked,
>   The middens of your burning beasts
>
> Shall be raked over till they yield
>   Last priceless slags for fashionings high,
> Ploughs to wake grass in every field,
>   Chisels men's hands to magnify.

Anyway, to get back to the story after this long digression, we did, in the end, fix the plumbing, and in doing so learnt the new-style plumbing art. We moved the Aga, which weighed the better part of a ton, to a concrete plinth we had made for it in what had been the 'drawing-room' and connected it to the existing chimney where it has never, to this day, worked really well. I have hauled holly bushes up that chimney, I have fired shot guns up it and down it, I have poured gallons of petrol down it and set light to it—I have done everything short of dynamiting it.

Now, the whole subject of cooking and heating is very complicated and open to endless discussion.

When we got to Fachongle Isaf there was a Rayburn in what had been the kitchen, with a crack right through it. The huge open chimney above it had been shuttered off with a piece of asbestos sheet through which an asbestos chimney poked. I ripped the broken Rayburn out, put a hammer into it, and sold it to a scrap-dealer. I ripped the asbestos sheet out and threw the chimney open to the stars again. We started lighting fires on the floor where the stove had been and found they smoked abominably. Then I learnt certain truths about open fires with big chimneys.

Firstly, an enormous amount of heat goes up the chimney to heat the sky. This we all know, but what many of us forget is

27

that in going up the chimney it takes a vast volume of air with it. This air has to come from somewhere and so it comes under the door, through the window frames, through the cracks in the ceiling above—anywhere it can. Now people find that this cold air hits them in the back of the neck as they cluster round the fire—so they put a sausage thing along the bottom of the door, seal the windows and the ceiling, etc. and then of course the fire goes out. Or it smoulders sulkily and smokes villainously.

The answer to this particular problem is to knock holes in the wall at the back of or side of the fire to the outer world. Then the replacement air can come from out there. You will still lose most of the heat of the fire up the chimney but at least you won't be smitten in the back of the neck. We did this and it sort of half worked—sometimes, if the wind is wrong, we get vicious gusts through the holes we have made and have to mask them with iron sheets—but *without* those holes life was unendurable.

Secondly, you should not try to burn wood fires on a grate. The wood simply blazes away and is gone in no time at all. You should dig an ash-pit, perhaps a foot or two deep, let it fill with ash, and burn your fire on top of this. If the fire goes out during the night the ash is still hot enough in the morning for you to be able to chuck a few dry sticks on, and off goes your fire again. Further, the fire burns slowly and steadily. The predecessors of our predecessors at the farm, we later heard, used a horse to drag huge oak logs in—the horse walking in by the front door and then through the door that led into the *gegin fach*. By that time the log was level with the fireplace and could be unhitched and lowered on to the fire with levers. The horse could then be backed out of the *gegin fach*, turned round in the kitchen and walked out of the front door again. George Hughes told me that once they tried this with a log that was too big and which lodged in the front door. The horse put his shoulders into the collar to try to shift the log—got it completely stuck—and then, of course, could not get out of the house himself. He started to relieve himself copiously while his owners fought to extricate the log. Finally they had to go and call George Hughes to bring *his* horse to drag the log out backwards and thus release the imprisoned animal.

Naturally any engineer would tell you that a fireplace such

as this is very inefficient. Well, of course no man should ever use the words efficient or inefficient without specifying *for what*. Efficient for converting wood into calories of used energy it is not—any more than a Gypsies' camp fire is. But supposing wood is *free?*

Anyway we have lived with our huge open fire for twelve years now, and have sworn at it, and cursed it, and coughed and choked when it has tried to smoke us out, and we have smoked bacon over it, and ham, and kippers, and salmon, and we have roasted sheep in front of it, and boiled soup over it, and grilled countless chops, and steaks, and salt herring on it, and sat in front of it to drink uncountable gallons of home-brewed beer, and told stories in front of it, and lies, and played music, and sung songs, and got drunk, and had quarrels, and made them up again, and maybe it is inefficient for converting wood into calories of energy but it has been very efficient at keeping a family happy, and quite a lot of other people too.

And here we come to a dilemma. I do not think that in our overcrowded world in which the fossil fuel is running out we can afford any longer the luxury of a smoking, stinking, ash-spewing, back-of-the-neck-freezing, open fire such as ours is (although we have enough wood on this farm to keep twenty such open fires going, and are still not able to keep pace with the growth of wood every year).

Fellow-freaks are constantly coming to me and saying: 'Why haven't you got a solar heat collector on your roof?' I always reply that I have the finest and most efficient solar heat collector in the world. Ten acres of woodland knocks any other solar heat system into a cocked hat. It grows much faster than I can cut it down.

We cannot, of course, all have ten acres of woodland; but as you go about these islands you see good firewood being wasted everywhere. Every autumn and winter smoke billows from a million fires, as hedge trimmings, timber slashings, tree tops, old stumps and all the rest are burnt. Even in our cities, where the restless city dweller is always pulling down old houses to put up worse ones, vast piles of timber rafters and planking and beams are burnt. The city man is no longer allowed to burn this sort of wood in his fireplace, so it is burnt on the demolition site, and the smoke goes up into the air just the same.

Until this massive waste is stopped nobody can reasonably say that these islands lack fuel.

However, I still do not think that we are justified in burning fuel in such a prodigal way as we do in our *simnai fawr*, or great chimney. When the planet Earth supported a reasonable number of people such chimneys were fine—but now that we have proliferated until we crawl like maggots on a dying sheep we must make better use of our resources. Well, last year we bought two stoves, made by Jotul of Norway, both extremely expensive, but both highly efficient. They are enclosed iron boxes, and the logs burn in a dead end so that they smoulder slowly, like burning cigarettes; an armful of small logs or even hedge-trimmings keeps them alight and giving warmth, they never go out unless you let them out, and they work very well indeed. What is needed now is for some small foundry in this country to develop similar stoves, so that people can buy them at a decent price. Meanwhile, I am working hard on improvising other efficient wood-burning appliances, but that is another story and belongs to another book. And to save myself an awful lot of correspondence let me say that you can get the Jotuls from: Simon Thorpe, Nant Brennin, Rhyd Lewis, Newcastle Emlyn, Cardiganshire.

But in those brave days we had not heard of Jotuls, or fuel shortages, and when I used to say (as I had been saying since I was a boy) 'one day the oil will run short' everybody rolled about laughing at me. Seymour singing his silly old song again. And so, as autumn set in, we kept a roaring fire blazing in our *simnai fawr*, and sat around it, when we had time to sit at all, in splendid atavistic comfort.

And we did most of our cooking on the Aga.

3 *We Meet Our Neighbours*

Before I go any further I must describe how we came to meet
our neighbours.

We didn't go out of our way to meet them, and they didn't
go out of their way to meet us. But the time came when our
grass was ready to be cut for hay. I can't remember how we cut
it: I think we got a contractor to do the job, and to bale it as
well. We didn't have a tractor in those days, and one horse will
not pull a grass-cutter.

We had no means of carrying the hay except in the Fish Van,
which only held about a dozen bales and there were hundreds of
them. The Whale, which still stood in the middle of our yard
like an enormous white elephant—we couldn't sell it—was too
large and unwieldy to get in our fields. So Sally and I went out
with the Fish Van, and started the laborious and apparently
hopeless task of carrying hay home in little dribs and drabs.

Then we heard the noise. It was a combination of tractor
engines and Welshmen singing. It got nearer, and two tractors
pulling two trailers came into our field, accompanied by about
a dozen people. They were singing. They had evidently been
at the beer.

They didn't come and speak to us. Used to English keeping-
oneself-to-one's-self I wondered if they had come into our
fields by mistake. Quickly they began to load the trailers, and
then drove away with full loads to the hay barn in our *haggar*,
or stack-yard. They unloaded the bales into the barn. I had gone
back with a van-load and got into the barn and stacked the hay.
It was very hard work. None of the men said anything to me all
this time. When the last bale was in the barn after perhaps a
dozen loads or so—'That's the one we were looking for!' was
the cry and the sweating men revealed the cause of their singing
—in the shape of two four-gallon stoneware crocks full of home

brew. Sally got mugs, we all sat down on the hay bales, and drank. And we sang. And we sang and we drank and so we went on until far into the night. We had met our neighbours. And we had been introduced to the local home brew which is the king of drinks. We soon managed to buy a *kive* (a big barrel with the top cut out of it) and learnt the art and mystery of home-brewing. Of course all farmers, all over England and Wales, at one time brewed beer, if they were any good. The practice was killed by wicked legislation and by the general tendency to do nothing for yourself and to become totally dependent on The Thing, but for some reason in our little corner of Wales the farmers still brew their own beer, and long may they continue to do so.

My Neighbours

The first time I ever met my neighbours
We'd cut two fields of hay, and had it baled.
We hadn't met a soul there up to that time
In that far Western land so foreign to us.
Sally and I began to cart this hay
In a little van. Oh hell! What labour!
Suddenly we heard the sound of singing
And tractor engines. 'They're coming here!
'Who the hell can they be?' And through our gate
Came tractors, two, and trailers, ten strong men
And gallons of beer, home-brewed, in jars.
Without a word, or by your leave, or coming near us
They loaded up our hay and off they took it
To our barn. And there unloaded it. And
Stacked it. I helped them, and the sweat ran down my chest.
'Thank you!' I said. 'Say "*Diolchh yn Fawr*" ' said one
I tried to say it 'Has missus mugs?' he said
She had. We sat down on some bales and drank
And sang. And then we drank some more. And sang
And drank some more. And sang. I'd met my neighbours.

While on this subject of beer (I'm afraid I digress—but this is a digressive book) I must describe the occasion on which I assisted the judge of the Home Brew Competition at Nevern Show to perform his office.

I had first come in contact with Nevern Show when I had been driving round Pembrokeshire looking for a farm to buy with my bank manager's money. I had rounded a corner of a narrow road and there below me lay a beautiful tree-bordered valley floor, with a river running through it, a fine little medieval church flanked by huge yew trees, and a small village. It was the loveliest natural setting imaginable. And on the valley floor was a small multitude of people—it was a field full of folk. It was Nevern Agricultural Show.

There was a pub over a fine arched stone bridge, and into this I went to find perhaps a dozen farmers, some of them oldish men, with their arms round each other's shoulders lustily singing very good songs, wonderfully harmonized, in Welsh. After a pint I wandered back across the bridge and went into the show ground, and looked at the fat cattle, and the big Friesian bulls, and the sheep and pigs, and the pretty girls on pretty horses. In the course of my wanderings I came to a tent, and it was a green tent and stood on green grass so that the sun, shining through the green canvas, and reflected from the green grass, made the two oldish men inside the tent look green too. It was a wonderful sight. The two men sat on packing cases and were tasting the contents of dozens of bottles of home-brewed beer. For this was the Home Brew Competition. Nor were they swilling the stuff around their palates and spitting it out, as the effete wine tasters do.

I went away to look at a farm, and then came back, and wandered into this show again. The place had a magic for me then as it has now. I came to the green tent and looked in. The two old men were lying flat out on the green grass, looking as green as ever, sleeping most peacefully. They were surrounded by bottles, scores of them, all of them empty.

Later the judging was moved to the School House, the home of a very good friend of mine named Vernon Jones, a school-master but really a poet and an artist, who is no mean taster of home brew himself. I witnessed there one dramatic announce-ment of the judges' findings. An expectant crowd waited outside the front door. The judgement was to be announced—by far the most important event at Nevern Show. The door opened, two men appeared, backed by a small crowd of helpers and

33

supporters, one of them announced First, Second and Third
Prizes in a firm voice, then both judges fell backwards, simul-
taneously, into the waiting arms of their helpers. They were
carried backwards into the house and the door was shut. There
was a loud cheer. Nobody could say they had not done their
duty.

My turn to assist at this grave ceremony came some years
later. Vernon Jones had been asked to be a co-judge with another
man, a Gwaun Valley farmer, but the latter withdrew at the
last moment because they had got his initials wrong in the
programme. Gwaun Valley men have their pride. Vernon asked
me if I would assist him, for the task was beyond the powers of
any one man.

We entered a room in Vernon's house in which there were two
chairs, a table with glasses, and bottles lined against the wall.

Then came the most demanding task.

The bottles were identical, with numbers on them.

'Try number twenty-six,' Vernon might say. 'It's maximalt.'

I tried it. 'Maximalt!'

'Out!' said Vernon. And the offending No. 26 was cast aside.
Maximalt was the name we gave to malt extract—as opposed
to the true, the blushful Hippocrene: real beer made from real
malted barley, sprouted and kilned and gently cracked and
mashed and brewed and barrelled.

'Try twenty-four,' Vernon might say. 'How does it compare
with eighteen?' Very like eighteen. 'Same brewer, I should say,'
would be Vernon's comment.

'Different brew though. Slightly rougher.'

'Strong though.'

'Strong.'

'Try a drop more.'

'Now it reminds me of another—was it Four or was it Six?'

'Have to try them.'

We tried Four. We tried Six. We tried Four again. Then we
tried Six. Then back to Twenty-four. Then Eighteen. Then
back to Four. Then back to Six. Which was best? Which was
second best? We measured no gravity, or alcohol content. Home-
brewed beer, of Nevern Show standard, has a colossal alcohol
content—you don't have to measure it.

And so we worked on, throughout the hot morning. From time to time we could see men peering anxiously in through the window at us. We loftily ignored them. There were two men in particular—two brothers from the Gwaun Valley—that home and shrine of home brew—one with a cloth cap and one with a trilby—whose heads kept appearing over a partition wall in front of the house. They gazed intently at us—but the moment they saw us returning their gaze their heads popped down again, out of sight. This became unnerving.

'Those two are brothers,' Vernon told me. 'They've been trying to get first prize for years and years. Never managed it. I've drunk beer in their house many times. I'll recognize it if I taste it.'

He did recognize it. It was like the nectar of the Gods.

'Try some more,' said Vernon. I tried some more.

Later we opened another bottle and tasted something very similar.

'I bet it's from those two brothers,' said Vernon. 'They often put two entries in.'

'But it's not the same brew,' I said.

'No—I should guess it's a month earlier. Try some.'

I tried some.

'Now try some of the other.'

I tried some of the other.

In the end we awarded these two beers—knowing they were brewed by the same hand—First and Second Prize. Third Prize, too, went to a noble beer. A boy staying in our house had smuggled (without me knowing) a bottle of our own beer into the competition. Vernon and I both recognized it immediately. It had to be rejected of course, because we judges were incorruptible.

We had to go through them all once or twice again, or at least the better ones, to make quite sure we were right in our judgement. Then the front door was thrown open and Vernon made his solemn announcement. Neither of us fell down. We stood like men, and like upright judges. The brothers who won First and Second were so overjoyed I thought they would both have strokes.

'Why did you give us *two* prizes?' they asked.

35

'Because they were different brews and they were the best two,' said Vernon.

'Yes—one we brewed in March and one in April.'

'There is only one thing to do now, John,' said Vernon, 'and that is to go to the beer tent and drink some English beer and sober up.'

And that is exactly what we did. The stuff tasted like weak, fizzy soda water compared to the noble liquor we had been drinking.

But it was the help with the hay-making that made us realize that in coming to this particular part of Wales we were coming into a very different sort of farming community from the one we had left.

I was made aware of this different spirit another time, on a filthy rainy day in the winter. A cow of ours had a difficult calving. I left her as long as I could, then I had to help her. I had to get a cord around the calf and haul it out. She had probably been lying there trying to calve for a long time before I found her and she was very weak.

She calved in a difficult place, on a steep slope, in very wet mud. I could by no means get her to her feet. Sally came and helped, and we hove and shoved, and slithered in the mud, and were drenched with rain, and every time we got her up she would flop down again, and we felt helpless.

Then we heard a tractor engine. Four of our neighbours appeared with a tractor which had a link-box on it (a sort of steel box) and they lifted the cow up bodily and put her in the link-box. They drove back to our cow-shed and we carried the cow inside, with her little calf. Mother and child recovered and both did well—if they had stayed on the wet hillside they would have died. One of our neighbours, Tom Howells (or Tom Brithdir as he is called because Brithdir is the name of his farm), had seen our struggles through his telescope and had summoned the others to our aid.

We have been able to return this sort of neighbourly help and kindness quite often: in fact this very day on which I write we have helped George Hughes, of Fachongle Ganol, get in his hay. The mutual hay-making is always done to the accompaniment of home brew, and the singing goes on far into the night.

This kind of activity puts a totally different meaning on the word *work*. This sort of work is fun and a delight—not something to be avoided, as most work done for The Thing is.

George Hughes's hay-making is different in kind from that of others because not only does Lil, George's wife, have home brew in the house, but George is apt to have smuggled several crocks of it out into the field too. Thus we have some to drink when we get back to the barn with a load—but then we have some more to drink when we get back to the field. We will not, in fact, either load or unload without this bonus. The time inevitably comes when we get back with a load and Lil comes out of the house to say the beer is finished.

We all sit down and solemnly refuse to touch a bale.

Lil goes back into the house and comes out again with a crock—which she proceeds to turn upside down. There is nothing in it.

We sit.

She brings another crock out, and demonstrates its emptiness.

We sit.

Finally she gives in and gets out another crock that is *full* and we have mugs all round. It is perhaps not surprising that often the last load of the day collapses.

You cannot live so closely concerned with your neighbours without occasionally getting into a feud with one. I once got into such a feud, and Dai and I would not talk to each other at all, although we laboured all day in George's hay field together, and, full of good home brew and mutual hatred, we happened to climb up on the last load home. The tractor started off and when it got to the steep place in the lane I had the awful feeling of the world beneath me in a state of total collapse. Like a bale of hay myself I sank into what I thought would be oblivion—and ended up completely buried in a great weight of hay bales.

I fought my way out—and when my head emerged into the air I saw another man fighting his way out. When he succeeded he and I were face to face—our noses not a foot away from each other. We both burst into gusts of raucous laughter—and how can you continue with a feud in conditions like that? So we loaded again, went back to George and Lil's house, and were singing together until far into the night.

But I am nearly always outside my neighbours' feuds. Not being related to anyone here I can stay neutral. This I believe is valuable to them, as well as to me, for I can often, by a word in here or there or a little bit of string-pulling, save a feud from getting worse. However, for a pastoral people, with bad fences and fence-breaking sheep, feuds are inevitable, and anyway they are part of the fun of living, and part of life, and it is better to feud occasionally with your neighbours than to ignore them (the worst thing you can do). In any case, I always notice that when a neighbour needs help the most feuding of his neighbours will give it to him.

George and Lil have five lovely daughters, all safely married, and not to rough farmers like George and myself but to men who, George told me pointing to his breast pocket, 'all have beeros—beeros—not dirty boots like we have—beeros!' Beeros means Biros—those ubiquitous ball-point pens, and George means by beeros that they don't have to work like we do but have clerical jobs—that you do with Biros—such as selling insurance. George is very proud of this.

George's daughters all have lovely voices, and so does their mother (who is much younger than George) and when the six of them sing together the result is a delight. George has a sister, older than himself but nevertheless very active, almost blind, and also given to singing songs—often very ancient and strange ones. It goes without saying of course that all the songs sung by our neighbours are sung in Welsh. The only two exceptions are a song that goes:

> Telephone to Glory
> Oh joy divine
> I hear the current coming down the line!

and another that rousingly exhorts us to:

> Bring them in!
> Bring them in!
> Bring them in from the fields of sin!
> Bring the wandering ones to Jesus!

But these are just sung, I feel, for the benefit of us *Saeson*—Saxons or English. Particularly the last one.

Lil sings a very lovely and moving song, the name of which in translation is 'The Black Chair of Birkenhead'. It is about the occasion when the bard who won the Chair at the National Eisteddfod—the highest honour to which a Welshman can aspire—was killed in the First World War, before he could claim his Chair, which was therefore draped in black and nobody sat in it. To hear Lil sing this song invariably makes me weep. George, like so many Welsh countrymen, is a poet, and has composed a fine song about all the places round about here including my farm. When he had his seventieth birthday, six years ago, a special ode was composed in his honour and ceremoniously read before him by Mansel Owen, the monumental mason, at the memorable party given in George's house.

There is something very *aristocratic* about such of my neighbours as are farmers. They belong to their land, just as their land belongs to them. Even though some of them are quite small men they seem larger than life—their land gives them an heroic quality. They are more than just Tom, Dick or Harry. They have great dignity. They are called, often, by the names of their farms: George Fachongle, Tom Brithdir, Willie Dolranog, Salmon Brithdir Bach, Willie Fynone. 'I am dying, Egypt!' has something of the same noble ring. On the opposite side of me from George, over a small river that is our boundary, in a fine old farmhouse—bigger than most—in the middle of a farm that is half woods, lives Brithdir with his very old mother, a fine and most aristocratic lady, his sister (neither Tom nor his sister is married) and a brother who is practically never seen by people outside the family. If you go there he takes to the woods. He is perfectly rational, very intelligent from all accounts, but just does not like to meet people. The only time I saw him in the open he flung down the hay-knife that he was sharpening and dashed into the woods. At night, in the winter, if you can get up to the house without alarming the dogs and thus alarming Garfield (the reticent brother) you can see all the family, the old lady and her three children, sitting round the fire singing most beautifully, for they all have magnificent voices. Garfield used to be famous for his singing and was much in demand for concerts, before he took to his strange retirement. Tom is the most gentle man I have ever met: I have never had anything

39

from him but helpfulness, kindness and good advice—and I can even forgive him when he brings me gifts, in the winter, of onions as big as my melons, shallots as big as my onions, leeks as big as my forearms and cabbages much bigger than even my head. But Garfield is the gardener, and used to win prizes in all the local shows, again until his retirement from the world.

Tom and I have many arrangements that work to our mutual advantage. Tom gave me a flock of sheep, the first year we came here. At least he lent me this flock of ewes—old ones, to be sure, and surplus of Tom's requirements for he is always very overstocked. The arrangement (a not uncommon one) was that Tom had the ram lambs that were born to the ewes, I had the ewe lambs, we split the wool, and when the ewes were finally sold off Tom had the money. Thus we were able to build up a good flock of sheep without laying out a penny. Now all the old ewes have gone and the flock belongs to us.

Working the other way, when Tom has been short of grazing, and we have had plenty, he has grazed his cattle on our land and paid us well for it. And in the winter of 1974–5 when every farmer was short of grass and hay and cattle were starving, Tom's mother was very ill and his cattle were literally storming through our boundary fence, so I cut off one of our marshes for their use (without telling Tom or charging him for it). Dave, my new son-in-law (but we are jumping in our story) and I and another helper or two completely rebuilt the common fence, not bothering Tom to help do it (as he legally and morally should have done) because he was so concerned with his old mother. Even the position of this fence is the result of friendly agreement between Brithdir and Fachongle Isaf. In places it is built well into Tom's side of the river, so my cattle have access to the water and to the shady trees beyond, to get away from the flies, and well into my side further down, so Tom's cattle have the same advantages.

But this fencing has in the past been something of a sore point (not with Tom, I hasten to add). We had one neighbour, new to a farm bordering us, and with whom we had not one yard of common fence, who gave me no peace because my sheep and cattle occasionally strayed across on to his land. I worked day after day on building a fence, having to hump all the material half a mile on my back from the nearest place the tractor could get to because it was deep in swamp-woodland, with no help from him, until one day Sally found one of his heifers, deep in our woodland, having trouble producing a calf. She got the calf out and then telephoned the neighbour to come and get the cow. The boot was on the other foot then and soon afterwards he turned up at my side when I was fencing and gave me a hand, and a stalwart hand too. And last year George Fachongle, whose farm was completely innocent of any scrap of fencing on its road frontage (his other neighbours had fenced his common boundaries with them) was nearly driven mad by his cattle getting out and grazing the *Cae Tir*—the Long Field; the road in other words. A fussy (our only fussy) neighbour kept telephoning the police about it. So Dave and John Greystone and I got to work and ran a fence right along George's road boundary for him. He provided the material—we did the work. George is seventy-six and his eyesight is not too good. In the world of The Thing, Nanny or the government would send George to a home for old people perhaps. Here his neighbours keep him farming by doing for him what he cannot do for himself, so that he can retain his home, livelihood and self-respect. Isn't that better than any damned 'Welfare Service'? And it costs nothing, except T.L.C., or Tender Loving Care, of people one for another. In a world organized along the lines that our valley is run on there would be no *need* for welfare services, nor for old age pensions, nor for any of *Nanny's* other trappings.

4 *Animals, Tame and Wild*

Work proceeded on all fronts, As for the buildings, they all, house included, had to be practically refurbished. New doors everywhere, new window frames, a new floor in the old granary so that I could use it as my writing room and Sally could share it as her pottery. We slid the electric kiln, which weighed perhaps half a ton and was very top-heavy, down baulks of timber from inside the belly of the Whale and walked it to the old mill-shed, which was below the granary.

We did a great deal of the work ourselves, but after a time we were helped by two very good craftsmen: a large, laughing man named Joe Cardiff, and Glasnant Morris who lived in a semi-bungalow he had built for himself just up the road. Joe was a professional carpenter and had come to us from Sussex while we were still living at the Broom, in Suffolk. He was full of intention to be a homesteader. He had a charming wife and two small children. With no money and rather bad luck he only questionably made it. He came to Pembrokeshire with us, bought a house and twenty acres up on a windy ridge near Crymych, at eight hundred feet and with a magnificent view, bought pigs and a cow and ducks: a fox ate the ducks, the cow eventually had to be sold, and I bought the pigs because they were not thriving and things were not going too well. They didn't thrive with me either.

Joe worked for us for a while, very much part-time and enormously hard, with a right good will, and was a delight to work with. Glasnant, whose name we shortened to Glas (*glas* means blue, *nant* means small stream) worked well too and, although a mason, would turn his hand to anything. We paid these two men the rate for the job and, although with their help we got a lot done, finding this money brought us very near to bankruptcy. For my usual source of income—writing and broad-

42

casting—came to an abrupt halt when we moved to Pembroke-shire. Instead of doing a cosy little five-minute talk or two for Radio Norwich of the BBC every week, and two or three fifteen-minute talks a month for London BBC, and the odd funny script for 'Monday Night at Home' and an occasional series of sound features, I worked on my new farm. Indeed, I see from my diary that I was working flat out during those rugged pioneering days on a book for which I had received a modest advance from the publishers, but which they kept for *five years* before they published it, during which time it brought me in no income at all.

When I look back I cannot see how Sally and I did it all. That was a most demanding book: I had to collate and make sense of a vast store of information and notes that I had compiled during months—years in fact—of research in East Anglia and I had to write it while three hundred miles away from my subject, and while my head was full of a thousand urgent and pressing matters connected with my new farm.

I see in the old diaries constant entries such as 'got the enemy cattle out of such and such a field.' Now the 'enemy cattle' weren't enemy cattle really—they just belonged to somebody else, but we did not want them on our land eating our grass. And 'getting them out' did not mean just driving them out (which we did every day, and several times a day), but keeping them out. By means of a new fence. A new fence that enclosed and secured another little section of our farm.

And I found that, in this stony new land of ours, fencing, like everything else, was much more difficult than it had been in Suffolk. The land was glacial till—rubble dumped there in the last Ice Age by glaciers—and there were stones, rocks, and boulders everywhere. In many places you might make a dozen abortive attempts before you got a post hole in the ground. I drive post holes with a very heavy steel bar and time after time I would drive the bar into the ground, only to strike rock, and strike it again, and then try to bust through it, or attempt to slam the boulder out of the way and get down beside it, and then try again and again, until the sweat poured down and I wondered if I ever was going to get a post in. But at least I knew how to put up wire fences, having learnt the trade in South West

43

Africa where the boundary fence of the average farm is four times seven miles long and where elephants are only one of the hazards a farm fence has to be built to take.

We started buying a cow here and there. Then we learnt a terrible lesson. Miranda, the pretty little Jersey that we should have left with the Watsons who loved her so, died of a disease called red water.

I had known red water very well indeed in Africa. I worked as a 'Livestock Officer' for the Northern Rhodesian Veterinary Department for several years, and red water was one of the most serious diseases of that country. But when Miranda got sick, didn't want to move at all—even when she began passing red urine—I never for a moment suspected a tropical disease. Red water I associated with the tropics, and with very hot and tick-infested parts of the tropics too. To think that you could find this exotic killing disease in cosy little Great Britain had never occurred to me: I would as soon have expected to find leprosy. I telephoned the vet too late; he came and injected, but poor little Miranda died.

Red water is caused by a protozoan unicellular animal which is carried by a tick. It can be checked by an injection of some chemical, followed immediately by the injection of another— which is to stimulate the heart which has been very nearly arrested by the effect of the first. Needless to say, after a dose of the virulent disease itself, and then the fearsome injections, the cow goes off milk if she is in milk, is very likely to abort her calf if she is carrying one, and loses dramatically in condition.

Local farmers let a cow go on for a day or two with red water before they inject her in the belief that 'it's good to let her rid herself of the poisons—then she won't get it again.' Of course what actually happens is that the cow builds up antibodies against the disease: if you inject her immediately the symptoms appear she won't do this. If cows are brought up from calves on a red water farm they don't get the disease: they carry an immunity. They are 'salted'.

Our cows that summer went down one by one with red water, but after Miranda I was ready every time with the syringe, which I kept myself. When the vet asked me if I could give an intravenous injection I told him I could. I didn't tell him I had sometimes given hundreds in a day.

It was one more anxiety though—one more thing to worry us. Another was practically incessant rain. We put the pigs (gilts) we had bought from Joe Cardiff behind an electric fence on the steep hill beside the house. A worse place we couldn't have found for them. Not only were they incessantly getting out but, as the rains fell, they wallowed in mud and mud began to flow down the hill. They remained thin and miserable. We had hoped to establish a vegetable garden on this steep south-facing slope. The pigs taught us that this was not to be. We were not used to farming on steep slopes and we didn't know about solifluction, or the propensity of soil to creep downhill. If we are ever to garden that slope we will have to terrace it.

Thinking that if we were going to have a boar we might as well have a good one, for a boar, like a bull, is 'half the herd', we went to a sale of some very fancy pigs of the Welsh breed. As at many auction sales around our way, home-brewed beer was dispensed in the farmhouse, as there is nothing like a pint or two of this to make the bidders bid. I bid up to sixty guineas for a noble boar: sixty guineas of my bank manager's money. We stuffed two straw bales into the Fish Van, to act as a barrier between the boar in the back and us in the front, hove the boar in behind them, leapt into the front seats with the object of getting the van moving so as to fling the boar off his feet and —lo and behold—the topmost straw bale landed on my head and nearly fell on my lap (it would have done if the steering wheel had not been in the way) and the boar thrust his very mean-looking head between Sally's and mine. His front trotters were on the hand brake and gear lever, his eyes had that crimson look about them that boars' eyes have when they are displeased with life, and he uttered fearful grunts.

'Hit him!' I said to Sally. 'Wallop him!' Sally picked up the starting handle, which happened to be under her feet, and walloped the pig. Meanwhile I was wrestling with the straw bale, trying to steer, walloping the pig, and swearing horribly. Whether he did not like the swearing or the walloping I don't know, but the boar withdrew, I slung the straw bale back over my head, Sally kept the boar at bay with the starting handle

45

and horrible oaths, and I drove the rest of the way with extreme recklessness—swerving to the left and the right very often so as to keep the animal off its feet.

Much later I had another travelling encounter with a pig, this time a sow—a beautiful Gloucester Old Spots named Sophie, and normally so tame that one could imagine taking her to bed with one. She had been away to a boar and a friend offered to fetch her home for me in his open truck. He had a tarpaulin over the truck and we hoped that this would keep the pig in. Unfortunately the owner of the boar had a sheep dog, and owners of sheep dogs (as of other dogs in fact) never seem to realize that *their* dogs need controlling. There was a rodeo, or wild-beast show, as dog chased pig round and round the yard. Eventually we collared the pig and flung her—by brute force— up into the back of the lorry and pulled the tarpaulin over her. But it was quite evident that no tarpaulin was going to keep the now enraged animal in. She would leap overboard and do herself a mischief.

'How are you going to keep her there?' said the farmer.

'I'm going to get in there with her,' I said. And I did.

Now a man has a moral superiority over a pig in that a pig will seldom attack him—and I *used* to think this was because we are superior beings to pigs. I now know that this is not so—the moral superiority is because we are *taller* than pigs. Get down on all fours—as I had to in order to get under that tarpaulin— and the pig has a moral, and a considerable physical, superiority over you. There I was, crawling about under this tarpaulin, and there was Sophie, enraged and frightened, and she wanted *out*! The lorry drove off—Sophie made for a weak place in the edge of the tarpaulin—I grabbed her by the hind leg and hauled her back. She turned on me baring her tushes, or knashers. Trying not to be out-done I bared my knashers, but mine, I realized, were small beer compared to Sophie's. Sophie charged me—and it was obvious from her demeanour that she charged with full intent to do me a bodily injury. Crouching under the tarpaulin I couldn't get out of the *way*. I lurched towards Sophie and shouted: *WOOF!* and whether it was this or the swinging of the lorry that threw her off her feet I don't know, but she turned and made for the other end of the lorry again. I found a piece of rope and managed to get a clove-hitch around Sophie's hind leg. With this I was able to prevent her from committing suicide and also keep her facing, for the most part, away from me. I thanked God every time our driver went round a corner, because inevitably Sophie would be flung off balance and I would get a respite. I was quite glad to reach home and get Sophie down to the ground, where she and I immediately resumed our friendly, placid relationship.

But to get back to those early days of the 'obstacle race'. One of the obstacles that presented itself was in connection with the simple matter of evacuating one's bowels. Months later we found that there was a *ty bach* (little house, or outdoor privy) in the middle of a tiny enclosed garden near the house but it was so overgrown with jungle that this edifice was invisible and we didn't know it was there. So we used to wander down into the woods every morning with a spade and dig a small hole. But wherever you tried to dig there was a rock. It would take perhaps half an hour to find a spot where you could dig a little hole. We had not yet learnt to distinguish between the places where there were rocks and the places where there weren't. Later our friends the Cleals lent us an Elsan, and of course the task of emptying this once a week fell to me, and again there was this difficulty of finding a place where one could dig. Later we built a septic tank. I got an estimate from the owner of a J.C.B. (that ubiquitous digging machine) to dig the hole for it (seven foot by seven by seven) and he wanted seventy pounds. I dug it by hand in a day, and thus learnt that it is possible to dig holes in rocky ground but that this involves very hard work. I had to haul boulders heavier than myself out of that pit. But at least when you hove such a boulder out it left a large space.

The whole question of sewage disposal needs a lot of thought. The fertility of North Africa went down the sewers of Rome, and the fertility of our own country is going down the sewers too and with it much of the fertility of America. It is monstrously wasteful to discharge sewage into the sea. On a national scale our government, if it had its priorities right, would put every other problem aside until it solved this most vital problem of getting human wastes back into the land again. But on the scale of a place like Fachongle Isaf—what is the solution there? If I knew

I would tell you. If you know—please tell me. But I don't know.
I know that our sewage now goes into this pit, seven foot by
seven by seven, and thereafter just disappears. It never fills the
pit up. It just goes. Presumably the useful nutrients in the sewage
flow out with water, and wastefully fertilize the jungle below—
I don't know—I only know I don't see them again. They don't
do my economy any good. There must be a way, and we should
not rest until we find it, of putting this marvellous fertilizer
back into the land. If it is objected that it is dangerous to use
it to manure crops that we thereafter eat—then we should use
it to manure crops that our animals eat. Personally I don't
think there is any danger either way: the soil is a marvellous ab-
sorber and breaker-down of all mortal remains, as gravediggers
know.

We are trying here now a device called the Wardha Latrine,
an invention of the Mahatma Gandhi, the first applied at his
ashram at Sevagram near Wardha in central India. I imagine the
one we are making is the first ever in Europe but I do not know.
You dig a trench—perhaps two foot deep—and half fill it with
waste vegetable matter. Leaves, bracken, spoiled hay—anything
will do. At one end of the trench you place a movable sentry box,
which has a lavatory seat inside it. When you have used this you
kick a little earth over the result, and when the trench has begun
to fill up you move the sentry box on a length and then fill in
the used bit of trench. When you get to the other end of the
trench you can move the sentry box sideways on to the end of
another trench. Now after three months if you dig out the contents
of the trench you find a sweet-smelling, friable, very valuable
fertilizer which your instincts will tell you will be safe to put on
anything. *Or*, you could leave the stuff where it is and plant
comfrey, or some other deep-rooting and greedy plant over it,
and perhaps use this for green manure. Either way the nutrients
in the sewage get back into the land, where they belong.

I have seen the Wardha latrine in use in India, and it works,
and works very well. I will know shortly whether it works in our
climate. But of course it involves, sometimes, a short walk, or
run, in the rain, and not many people nowadays will put up with
that. If you *have* an indoor latrine, with a pull-and-let-go system,
you will find a great temptation to use it, particularly on a rainy

day. In the event, as the sentry box was thatched with grass, the cows ate it.

Well, we got our pull-and-let-go system, our bathroom with tiles decorated by Sally and embellished with two most sexy mermaids (the mermaid's tail starts well *below* the belly-button— did you know?) and a big fish about to swallow a smaller fish; the Aga worked; we moved into the house from the yard and began to do the cooking inside, and gradually the practical business of housekeeping became routine and took up less time. But right from the start at Fachongle Isaf we had more than a conventional family has to do. There were hens, ducks and geese to be let out and fed, and a cow to be milked in the morning; then the milk had either to be put through the separator or else left to set in the setting-pans for the cream to rise; we had to 'fleet' or skim the previous day's milk and scald and clean milk-buckets, separator or setting-pans. We baked our own bread (we use to buy wholemeal flour then from a mill the other side of Carmarthen; now we grow wheat most years or buy in bulk from a farmer if we don't for some reason, and grind it ourselves). We also made butter and soft cheese, and sometimes hard cheese as well when there was a surplus of milk, although this involves a lot of work. There were various country wines to make, and it was not long before we slipped in the custom of our Welsh farming neighbours and began to brew beer. And the brewing of beer (properly, from real malt which comes in a sack and is simply sprouted barley—not sticky stuff you buy at the chemists) changes your life.

The countryside was infested with foxes, and so I built a large pen for the geese. I enclosed part of a stream with a high wire-netting fence supported on long alder poles. I knew the alder poles would only last for a year or two, because the stuff rots in the ground; but nothing else was readily available and I was buying time. The pen also enclosed some rough grass and a wooded bank. How innocent I was! Our Pembrokeshire foxes will get through almost *anything*. They waited until the geese were sitting on their eggs, and had been so sitting for long enough nearly to bring them off, and then they came in and wantonly destroyed them. They killed the gander too for good measure. I built a hen-run on the other side of the house, on an island

ANIMALS, TAME AND WILD

between two small streams. First the foxes got in—in *spite* of the fact that I buried the wire-netting a foot deep. I tried various remedies. One was to have a little dog on a short chain which was stapled to a wire in the pen. This kept the foxes away but the little dog didn't like it and used to howl. The second was to put electric fence wire right round the pen at fox-nose level. This kept the foxes away but it did not keep out two mink (mink have escaped from fur farms and spread over the country) and they were worse than the foxes. I telephoned the Ministry of Agriculture and they sent a mink-man who successfully set down traps.

The foxes have never allowed us to keep geese. We have tried three times and every time the foxes have killed them all. They seem to love geese so much that they will dare *anything*, go through any obstacle, to get at them. The foxes are getting worse, every year more lambs are lost to them by ourselves and our neighbours and this year, for the first time, we cannot let hens run out on free range—they are taken in broad daylight within yards of the house.

You may ask—why don't you shoot the foxes? Well, we do when we get the chance, but I spent five consecutive afternoons sitting in a hide within rifle range of some free-range hens and never saw a fox. On the sixth day I didn't sit there and the fox killed three hens. And, in a busy life, there is a limit to the number of afternoons you can spend sitting up for foxes. When we do shoot a fox it is generally quite unexpectedly. Sally, who is a dead shot with a 'two-two', has shot two or three with it, and I once shot one through the window of the house with a shot-gun. My greatest triumph in the dastardly art of vulpicide was when some fifty members of the local Fox Society came to the farm. It was a pouring wet day and they asked me if they could hunt the farm. I said they could and they slogged about for several hours in our swamp-jungle, and in Brithdir's over the river, with no result. They then came to me to borrow a spade, for they had put terriers down some earths on my farm and wanted to dig them out. I lent them a spade and walked up with them, to a long row of earths at the bottom edge of Parc Clofas, just in the wood. No sooner had I got there than a big dog fox broke out of an earth and ran into the wood. Four shots rang out from four shot-guns, the owners of which were standing just behind the hole—followed by four more shots as they emptied their second barrels. The fox ran away unscathed. This, I thought, is ridiculous, and I went back to the house and got my own modest cheap Spanish single-barrelled gun. Everybody had forgotten about the foxes, and were all standing about in groups talking when Tom Brithdir, who did not have a gun, touched my arm and pointed behind me. A vixen was very quietly moving out into the wood. I shot her, and I don't think some of those stalwart hunting men, who were soaking wet and covered in thorns after a day in the rain forest without having got anything, have yet forgiven me.

I don't think any real countryman would like to see foxes exterminated. Their presence adds some mystery and wildness to our lives. We secretly admire their cunning, and when we tell each other the story of their latest depredation our indignation is mixed with a certain excitement and—well, envy almost—for after all there is a wild wicked predator deep down in every one of us trying to get out.

The city man's current concern that foxes should not be hunted always surprises me. It is cruel to hunt a fox, he says. Well then—isn't it cruel when a fox tears my poor old mother-goose off the eggs she was just going to hatch out—after she could even feel the stirrings of the little chicks within them? Ah, but that's natural, says the townsman. Well, I reply, then it is natural for me to hunt foxes—I am natural too. The fox, that great hunter, can hardly complain if he is hunted as well. But he doesn't complain—he just uses all his wit and cunning and stamina to escape, and turns and fights valiantly and desperately at the last when hope has gone. That is why we admire him even though we hate his guts.

What we need here is a 'farmers' pack'. Once when I was filming in North Wales I went out with such an arrangement. Someone lent me a shot-gun, I crawled into the back of somebody else's van which I shared with a couple of other armed men and some terriers, and we drove up into the mountains, on which was a light covering of snow. We came to a remote block of forestry plantation, got out, and joined perhaps fifty other people, all carrying shot-guns, some hung with bandoleers, and all bearing a superficial resemblance, in that wild mountain setting, to an army of bandits. A large van drove up, a young man wearing hunting green got out of it, with a whip and a horn, opened the back and twenty couple of fine hounds leapt out.

We ringed the wood, the hounds were put in, we could hear great music being made in the thick wood for some time and then a fox broke out and was shot by a man high up the mountain over on my right. We walked miles over rugged mountains that day and killed four foxes. 'That makes seventy-four for the season,' a man told me. He told me that he hunted twice a week all winter.

'How can you afford the time?' I asked.

'I cannot *not* afford the time,' he said. 'A good fox-kill means a good lambing average. One year when we only killed about thirty in the season we lost hundreds of lambs about here. We must try and kill over a hundred—then we only lose a few lambs and that we don't grudge.'

I asked him if he would like foxes to be exterminated.

'Of course not—they are part of the mountains, aren't they? We and foxes can live together—but we have to keep them down. Otherwise our livelihood is gone. It is them or us.'

And that is the way of it. If fox hunting was abolished in these wild places, cyanide gas and strychnine would be used, and the fox would be completely exterminated, which would be a great mistake.

A mistake partly for moral reasons—man has no right to destroy a species of fellow animal. But also for practical reasons. I am now able to plant young trees every year at Fachongle Isaf without the huge expense of rabbit fencing. Myxamotosis got the rabbits down—but it is the foxes which *keep* them down. I believe that we will never suffer a severe infestation of rabbits again as long as we have got foxes. Why did we suffer from such an infestation before we had myxomatosis? Well, for a very simple reason. In pre-myxomatosis days a ubiquitous fellow in most parts of the country was the rabbit-trapper. During the Great Depression trapping rabbits yielded the greater part of the living of most of the farmers ar ound here. The gin trap, now illegal, was the engine for taking rabbits and these were set in hundreds of thousands about the countryside. And not only did

they kill rabbits—they killed foxes too and they killed them by
the thousand. In gin-trap days foxes were no problem—but rabbits were. The very engine intended to control the rabbits helped
protect them—for it killed the rabbit's most active predator.
Now rabbits are gone, foxes are back, and Man must take a
controlling hand himself. He is, or should be, the Good Husbandman. He should see that every species of plant and animal gets a
fair deal, that none gets too numerous and oppressive, and that
a good balance of nature (and Man is part of nature) be preserved.
Oh yes—we must control our own numbers too.

Another creature that we had many of is the badger. My first
sight of a badger here was when one of the children, waiting up
on the road for the school bus, came running back to say that a
badger was caught in a snare in the hedge on the roadside. I got
a pair of pliers and walked up to look. And behold, a badger was
indeed in a snare which was around his fat belly and he was
absolutely furious. I have never seen an angrier badger. I cut a
forked stick and, with great difficulty and some danger of being
bitten, held the badger down with this and cut the wire. He gave
me a reproachful look over his shoulder—then waddled off across
the field in a great hurry and looking very comical. I felt as I
watched him that, whatever I did in my life, I could never kill a
badger. The man who had set the snare though, when told that
I had cut it, announced that I was a 'bloody fool'. This I was
later told by Glas.

'Why?' I asked.

'They roll on oats. They are a nuisance.'

'Roll on oats? What utter bloody rubbish.'

'You'll see, when your oats are ripe,' said Glas.

We had planted Parc y Banc Isaf, a field near the house, with
oats. I forgot all about the badger theory, forgot about the oats
in fact, until one day Tom Brithdir came over to me and said:
'The badgers have started on your oats.'

'What do you mean?' I said.

'I can see your fields from my house better than you can,'
said Tom. 'You go and look.'

Tom and I went to the oat field and found a terrible mess.
Perhaps a quarter of an acre was completely flat, there were
runs flattened down in the rest of it and there were badger

droppings everywhere. Tom said no one knew why they did it: some said it was to scratch themselves; some said they just loved to play in the growing corn; some said they knocked it down so as to eat the grain. Indeed, we found oat husks in their droppings so we knew that some of the corn was eaten, but obviously more than this was needed to explain the extent of the damage.

That night I went out with a shot-gun and crept silently along the boundary between the oat field and the wood. I heard a great rustling out there. That's no badger—that's a large flock of sheep, I thought. I walked into the oats with the intention of chasing the sheep out—and was nearly knocked over by a badger charging past me—right by my legs. As I had given up the idea of badgers and was thinking of sheep I was not ready with my gun and did not shoot. Then all around me was the sound of rushing badgers. There must have been thirty of them in the field that night!

Next day I borrowed a reaper and binder and harvested the oats prematurely. It would be too green to thresh but we could feed it in the sheaf. It was very difficult to harvest, as the badgers had made such a mess of it.

I don't know what to do about the problem of badgers. Several of my neighbours have given up growing corn because of them (they attack wheat and barley as well as oats, but not so badly). It is sad to have to give up corn-growing in a hungry world. I have thought of badger-high electric fencing (but haven't tried it yet) or of sleeping in a tent in the field at night. Again, in the days of the gin-trap (the only really effective trap that has ever been invented, and I imagine the only possible one) badgers were severely controlled. I don't want to see the gin-trap reintroduced. A law has just been passed making it illegal to hunt badgers. I resent all laws passed by city people (as all laws are) to control the actions of country people. The only mitigating circumstance about them is that they are almost always unenforceable.

We have far more predators in Wales than one commonly sees in England. There is generally at least one buzzard soaring up in the sky over my farm—often two. When there are two they talk to each other with weird, high-pitched screaming noises. There are plenty of owls, and not a few sparrow hawks and kestrels, also weasels and stoats. The result is that we are very free of the sort of animals that damage crops; pigeons, rabbits, hares, pheasants, partridges. There are no hares at all—I have been told by one of my older neighbours that he has never seen a hare in his life.

Of the dogs we brought over from England with us you will remember Esau, the most splendid lurcher that ever lived. In Suffolk he was known to run down and kill three hares in a morning, which is an exceptional feat for any dog. In Pembroke-shire he was lost. He just could not understand a countryside that had no hares in it. He took to going down fox earths and ranging the hills chasing foxes. I tried to keep him at home, but he became (as some dogs do) uncontrollable. Short of keeping him chained up all the time we could not keep him at home. One day he went away—and never came back again. I thought he had been shot by a farmer, but months afterwards I found his mummified body hanging from a wire fence: he had tried to jump it but had got his hind toes caught in the top two wires.

Nearly every farmer round here will shoot any dog not his own he sees on his land, sling the carcase into the woods for the foxes to eat and then say nothing about it: what the ear doesn't hear the heart doesn't grieve about. The owner of the dog simply knows that he has lost his dog—he never knows who shot it. This may sound ruthless, but we hadn't been living here very long before we found out the reason for it. Dogs chase sheep. I think I am right in saying that *all* dogs, given the chance, chase sheep. I have had to shoot two of Sheba's pups in my life, which I was rearing up to be sheep dogs, because they were caught red-mouthed by neighbours killing sheep. One year I lost seven lambs—fat and ready for the butcher—to dogs. I found them, all in one day, torn to pieces.

Tom Brithdir, that reliable friend, came over to me and told me that he had been watching three dogs chasing my sheep, through his telescope. He knew whose dogs they were. He came with me and we confronted the owner of the dogs.

'My dogs *never* chase sheep,' he said. We all say that. 'I let them out to hunt foxes down in the woods.'

'Possibly they find sheep a more rewarding quarry than foxes,' I said. In the end we convinced him (Tom's evidence was

ANIMALS, TAME AND WILD

crucial) and he paid for the sheep and shot the dogs. He was a good neighbour. If he had refused to pay I would have sunk into even worse financial trouble than I was then in. Tom Brithdir lost eleven lambs last spring. He caught the dog (a corgi) but the owner was a poor woman who could not afford to pay so Tom lost over a hundred pounds of hard-earned money.

The climax in the dog-war came last winter. Peter Lloyd (the son of the man whose dogs killed my sheep) rang me up to say that there were a dozen dead and dying sheep on his land—would I like to have some of the mutton? I went over and Peter and I drove out, and had a grisly hour or two running down sheep which had their faces hanging down under their chins, cutting their throats with a pen-knife, checking them into the Landrover and driving them back to Peter's farm. Next day there were another dozen. At night we patrolled with shot-guns—during the day we finished off, skinned and gutted sheep. All ewes with lambs in their bellies.

Everyone's dog was suspect. No owner of a dog will ever believe that his darling pet has killed sheep. One particular huge dog was seen three times actually worrying sheep—but each time the owner was accused he swore blind the dog had been locked up at the time. Every night the depredations grew worse—sheep on half a dozen farms were attacked until in the end over two hundred had been killed or mauled so that they had to be finished off. It was sad and revolting and one's heart sank at each day's news. Finally the whole countryside was mustered, the police force was called out (they used our farm as H.Q.), a great drive was organized, two dogs were shot red-mouthed, another traced down to its owner and later shot, and the battle was over. It had cost my neighbours perhaps four thousand pounds which they could not afford, caused untold suffering to two hundred sheep, caused we don't know what damage to unborn lambs, and killed three dogs. No wonder sheep farmers don't like other people's dogs and get infuriated when some dog-owner says: 'My dog would *never* chase sheep!' *All* dogs will chase sheep—there is not a dog in the world which will not chase them if encouraged by another dog and taught how to. In this country there are *far too many dogs*! A mountain sheep farmer must have one or more working sheep dogs but any dogs in excess of this, in sheep country, are a menace and should not be there at all. All right, I have a puppy now, but he's a fat Labrador puppy and will shortly be a fat Labrador dog and will never chase sheep at all. Or will he?

Sally once looked out of the kitchen window and saw an Alsatian dog chewing the leg of a live sheep in our orchard! She went out with the rifle, caught the Alsatian and tied him up, and shot the sheep. If I had been there I would have shot the dog too and made an end of it. The Alsatian thereupon broke his chain again and lit off home. Sally telephoned the police, they came out, went to the house of the dog's owner, and confronted him with the news. The owner (of course) said: '*My* dog would never chase sheep—in any case he's chained up.' They went round the back and there was the dog with a broken chain and blood all over him. Even then the owner had to be threatened with court proceedings before he agreed to have the dog destroyed.

Our old sheep dog bitch, Sheba, had countless pups. We managed to place the first litter of these with local sheep farmers, and they acquired such a good reputation that we never had any difficulty later in selling or giving away her puppies to farmers. Her progeny are easily recognizable, and it is pleasing to go about the country and constantly be spotting—often in some far-off parish—dogs that are obviously Sheba's—her grandchildren if not her children. Alas, she was destroyed, last year, at the age of about fifteen, by being run over by a car-lout, and it was this event that started me off writing this book. For I felt that an era—a natural period of my life—had come to an end.

5   *Farming Matters*

During eight years of homesteading in Suffolk Sally and I had come to the conclusion that it was better not to engage in very much commercial activity. That is, she potted, I wrote, both very much half-time, we grew the food that we ate, did our own building, making things and repairing things, and only sold the produce of our five acres of land when we had a natural surplus that we didn't know what to do with. It worked out that what we received for surplus weaner pigs for example, or surplus calves, just about paid our bill at the mill for feeding-stuffs that we were unable to grow on our small acreage.

True, the sow herd eventually became predominantly commercial, for we only needed three weaner pigs a year to fatten for our own use and we built up to six sows which gave us well over a hundred weaners a year and these of course we sold. But the difficulty that all small sow-keepers have is getting their few sows in pig (pregnant). It is not economic to feed a boar to serve just one sow for example (he performs his office only twice a year and yet you have to keep him, fairly expensively, all the time). Six sows, I think, is the minimum number that will 'pay the wages' of one boar. Therefore we either had to use a 'boar-walker' or keep six sows. There was a boar-walker in Ipswich. When we kept only one or two sows we did use his boar. We would telephone him, he would arrive in a van, open the back, an enormous boar would waddle out, follow his master to the expectant sow, perform his office with a sort of blasé indifference, grunt, turn round, walk unbidden into the van again and wait for the door to be shut. The love life of pigs is far less complicated emotionally than ours is. The problem, though, was for us to spot the sow during that brief period when she needed the boar. If we were busy, or away, or unobservant, we would miss her and fail to send for the boar at the right moment.

So we started keeping six sows and our own boar and saved these troubles. And in fact, the sow herd always paid us. Viewed solely as a commercial venture it was a very successful one. (A trap that farmers fall into is to say such things as: 'Six sows are paying me well. Six hundred will pay me a hundred times as much.' They won't.) But six sows paid us very well. We grew fodder beet (the best of all easily-grown non-graminous pig feed) and Jerusalem artichokes for them, threw them all the waste vegetable matter from the garden and slops from the kitchen, bought tons of 'stock-feed potatoes' and 'stock-feed carrots' and threw these to them raw (pigs like cooked potatoes but will put up with raw ones too, their philosophy being that life would be rawer if there weren't any). Stock-feed potatoes were perfectly good ware potatoes (ware means fit to sell for humans) that were surplus to the Potato Marketing Board's requirements. In the chaos that resulted from the setting up of yet another government-sponsored 'marketing board' hundreds of thousands of tons of potatoes were allowed to rot in the clamp after they had been paid for. We were the beneficiaries of this bureaucratic lunacy and we could buy tons of fine potatoes at ten shillings a ton. Sometimes we had to supplement this almost free food by barley meal from the Mill. But the money we got from selling our weaners (weaners are pigs that have just been weaned—we used to sell them between eight and twelve weeks old) more than paid for these inputs and left a very handsome profit. In fact, many a time a cheque for weaners arrived just in time to save us from acute financial embarrassment. Further—a thing most farmers don't think of—all the feeding-stuffs we imported into the farm *stayed there in the form of fertility*. It is this fact that makes nonsense of the statement that feeding grain to animals to make meat is 'inefficient' because only such-and-such a percentage of the food-value of the grain is turned into meat. Of food fed to animals *nothing* is wasted. If you take vegetable matter and put it in a compost heap, in three or four months you will have good compost. If you put it in a pig instead of a compost heap—in a few *hours* you will have even better compost. Every time, at the Broom, that I bought a bag of barley meal, or a ton of spuds or carrots, or a ton of hay (we very seldom had to buy hay, though) I knew that I was buying in somebody else's fertility. Thus in eight years our five acres improved from land about as barren as land can be in England and not blow away, into land of very high fertility.

But we are miles away from our farming matters at Fachongle Isaf in Wales. Just three hundred and forty-five miles away in fact.

At Fachongle Isaf we got inveigled into commercial farming. There we were, with a farm of seventy-four acres at that time and a huge overdraft, and we felt we had got to farm. Further, we joined a thing called the Small Farm Scheme, run by the Ministry of Agriculture. If you belonged to this you had to improve your farm as they told you, increase the stocking rate of various animals at the rate mutually agreed upon, and in return they gave you—yes *gave* you—dribs and drabs of money.

Featherbedding the farmers of course. Yes—and they *needed* featherbedding. Since the repeal of the Corn Laws in 1846 the policy of successive English governments has been quite simple. It is to impose heavy import duties on all manufactured foreign goods but to allow complete free trade in agricultural produce. The effect of this simple policy is also quite simple. It is to make the farmers (and in fact all countrymen who are people dependent on agriculture in one way or another for their living) pay more for everything they need from the towns (because British industry, being sheltered by tariffs, has always been comparatively inefficient) but to ensure that the countryman gets the least possible return for what he produces (because his produce is exposed to the competition of the entire world). This is what is known as 'the cheap food policy'. It has meant that farmers and farm workers have always been the hardest worked but lowest paid people in this country (even now, after several reforms, the minimum agricultural wage is the lowest wage earned by anyone and the income of the average farmer is *lower* than the minimum agricultural wage). It has also meant the depopulation of the countryside, the demoralization of country people, a feeling of inferiority among them which they should not have (they deserve a feeling of superiority), the introduction of cruel and harmful methods of agriculture, and the rape of the Earth. The townsman has got his cheap food of course, but the sands are running out on him. Soon he

60

will be lucky to have any food at all. I find I am forced to quote yet again that stinging little verse by a countryman, Ralph Hodgson:

> I saw in a Vision
> The Worm in the Wheat
> And in the shops nothing
> For people to eat
> Nothing for sale
> In Stupidity Street.

The issue is obscured by the fact that as thousands of farmers have been driven out of business and farm workers ejected from their jobs, land has been grabbed into huge units by greedy financiers. These men have become very rich (for if you can make a bare living on fifty acres you must, helped by machines and chemicals, be able to make a fortune on five thousand) and so people, seeing these entrepreneurs, think: wealthy farmers. But the *real* farmers—the men who, with skill and traditional knowledge can really *feed* this country, by growing plenty of good food with *a low input of imported and oil-derived chemicals*—don't make a good living. They are poor, grossly overworked, and sneered at by lesser men.

So I had no scruples about accepting the small amounts of money the city man handed out to me provided that I danced to his or his agent's particular tune. The trouble was that this tune came very near to breaking me—as it did many another small farmer. I felt like saying then, as I feel like saying now, and as most other farmers would say: 'Give us a fair price for our produce, or at least allow it to find its own market price—and you can keep all your dribs and drabs of charity!' It is rumoured of a neighbour of mine that on going to chapel and finding an English-speaking parson officiating, he fell asleep, and that in the middle of the prayers, when the parson was saying: 'Grant we beseech Thee' he woke up, shook his wife, and said 'What's that about a Grant?'

Why should the farmer, the one man upon whose back *all* other people in the country ride, the man who feeds everybody, have to depend on charity? The remedy is clearly to be seen. The farmer, like the miner and electricity worker and civil servant and all the other classes of workers, should withhold his labour. Milk makes a fine fertilizer—on to the land with it. Eggs do too—smash 'em—on to the land. Then, the farmer should farm just for himself and the people in his own village and immediate neighbourhood. Let the cities get their food from abroad—if they can. If they can't, let them go without for a while. It wouldn't take many days of 'industrial action' of this kind to make the city man see the same sort of reason that he saw when his coal was cut off, or his power, or his rail transport, or any other of the services and commodities that he finds so important.

But unfortunately the farmer has sold himself body and soul to The Thing that is now oppressing him, and also any true husbandman finds something blasphemous about destroying good food. So I signed up for the Small Farm Scheme, and had to 'drastically harrow, and apply lime and slag' to field after field, slowly increase our stock of cattle, sheep and pigs to the agreed numbers year by year, and also (and this is where we went wrong) go in for a grandiose draining scheme in the marshes.

We got a contractor to dig the ditches and 'tile drain' trenches necessary with that ubiquitous tool—a J.C.B. These letters stand for the man who started the firm that makes them, but a J.C.B. is a big yellow tractor with a dozer blade on one end and a digger on the other. To see one operated by an expert is a revelation: the thing looks like a live animal grazing in the swamp land, picking up a mouthful here and dumping it there, lifting itself up on its four feet to get a firmer stance for its job, withdrawing its feet into its body and crawling forward on its huge wheels and—whenever it gets stuck in the mud or sunk in a swamp—hauling itself out to harder land with its own digger.

The J.C.B. dug an open ditch round Waun Fach, and I got a man with a tractor to plough this field and re-seed it. The same with Parc y Bardd. Glas ploughed that with a tractor he borrowed from his neighbour. These re-seedings were only partially successful: Waun Fach soon returned to marsh again although Parc y Bardd became a moderately decent field. (We have drained it further since I wrote the above and it is now quite dry.)

But it was down in the two four-acre marshes in the heart of our farm that the J.C.B. really showed its paces. It started there in the middle of a very wet winter—and I have seen it half-buried in wet peat and mud and yet manage to claw itself out by pushing behind with its dozer blade, pulling in front with its wildly grabbing digger arm, the two huge wheels meanwhile spinning madly in the mud to help. Suddenly the huge thing would tip and lurch and roll forward—only to wallow into another apparently bottomless mud-hole. I did not realize that such marshes should only be tackled in the summertime, and none of my advisers bothered to tell me. The contractor was happy to have his machine working at all in the winter, and the mess he was making of my marshes meant nothing to him. The driver of the J.C.B., a small lively man named Gwyn Bach, was nothing less than a genius.

The J.C.B. dug open ditches around the top contours of the two big marshes, and the contractor had these ditches fenced as this was part of the contract and insisted upon by the Ministry of Agriculture. It would have been better to have left them unfenced. The fences were to keep cattle out—which they didn't; all they did was to make it difficult for me to flash out (cut the vegetation from) and clean out the ditches in later years. The J.C.B. then dug two trenches across each marsh, 'tile drains' (earthenware pipes) were laid in the trenches, a back-fill of small stones was put on the pipes, and the J.C.B. pushed the earth back on top of the back-fill.

The result of all this was to half-drain the marshes, and nearly to break me. For although the government paid about half the cost of the operation I had to pay the other half, which came to well over a thousand pounds. I didn't have a thousand pounds, but by then we had at least reared up eight fine bullocks, worth a hundred pounds apiece, and these we simply handed over to the contractor, thereby cancelling out most of the debt. But I had been banking on the sale of the eight bullocks to pay off a lot of other debts too.

Sally and I are what the Americans call 'highly motivated people'. We are not content to sit and watch the world go by. We always want to 'do different' as they say in Suffolk. If we had gone quietly ahead with making ourselves self-sufficient in food, which would have meant having two cows and their off-spring, killing three pigs a year, and keeping a couple of dozen fowls and a few other things, while Sally had got on with her potting and I with my writing, life would have been perfectly comfortable, we would have paid off our not inconsiderable overdraft in the ripeness of time, and died happy. As it was, we rushed at farming like a bull at a gate. The marshes had to be drained—*immediately*. A beef herd had to be built up—*immediately*. The forests had to be cleared, the boundaries fenced, the gaps gated, the house made comfortable, the buildings repaired, poultry runs made, pig houses built, a sheep flock established, a sheep-dip built, all *immediately*. And at the same time Sally had to pot and I had to write to pay for it all.

It was impossible. What we were trying to do was quite impossible.

The man farming a thousand acres in the Eastern Counties will say: why on earth should it be impossible for a man and his wife, even though both are working half-time, to run a seventy-four-acre farm? Here I am, with old Charlie and young Bert to help me, making a very good profit out of a thousand acres and we have time to spare!

The two things are just not comparable. The Eastern Counties farmer has no animals for a start, and so not a moment a day is taken up by looking after them. And having no animals he needs no fencing. Now even if I had no animals I would still need fencing—to keep *other* people's animals out. You may say that legally they should keep their own animals in, but in practice they don't. The English arable farmer has hardly any hedges or ditches. He has piped the ditches and filled them in, he has bulldozed the hedges out. So, no ditch-cleaning or hedge-trimming. He has none of the jobs the arable farmer used to have to do by hand—selective weed poisons save him from hoeing; the combine harvester, potato harvester and sugar-beet harvester save him from any hand work at all with the harvest; huge tractors pulling multi-shared ploughs and other implements do his cultivation. Virtually all the work of the farm is done from the seat of a tractor and all building and repair maintenance work is done by contractors from outside.

What an efficient method of farming, you may say. But reflect: the input of oil, chemicals, machinery, and contractor-effort going into that thousand-acre farm is enormous. Every crop is sprayed several times (it is not unusual now for corn to be subjected to five or six sprays during its period of growth—and an orchard gets a dozen sprays a year!) and *each one* of these sprays costs more than the whole of the land would have in 1930. Each tractor—and the arable farmer will have several—will have cost at least four thousand pounds (a combine harvester may well cost eight thousand) and these enormously powerful and sophisticated machines do not last long. They may save labour on the farm, but look at the colossal amount of labour it takes to build them! There might only be two men working on that thousand acres—but there is a hidden labour force of tens of thousands working part-time for that farm in other places. Why, two thousand feet underground in Zambia there are men mining copper to help build those machines, and oil drillers and roustabouts are sweating it out in the desert and on the North Sea to provide the oil which is the basis of all those chemicals.

Sally and I worked, not with the four-thousand-pound tractor and the poison spray, but with the axe, the slasher, the spade, the hoe, the saw and hammer and chisel. Sally has always been amazingly proficient with tools, although I have yet to meet a woman who is good with a felling axe. I had already developed, and continue to develop, skill with all the outdoor tools. I would be a dismal failure as a cabinet maker but when men not so used to it come and help me fell trees I can generally knock down four or five to their one.

I felled acres of trees the first winter we were at Fachongle. I tried hard to clear the two big marshes in the centre of the farm, over which the alder copse was creeping out from the wetter parts at the bottom to cover the whole field. Much of our ten-acre wood was shown as open land on the 1904 map. Now it was high jungle. Alder grows astonishingly quickly and it is very hard to clear it short of dragging it out by the roots with some machine. I felled the trees, hacked off and burnt the branches, and carried the trunks back to the house to feed the insatiable *semnai fawr* or big chimney. There was no way of getting those trees out except by carrying them on my shoulder for several hundred yards over extremely wet boggy and uneven ground through a mass of brambles.

The result of all this activity can be seen now, and is to our benefit, but at that time it was misplaced effort. An under-capitalized new farmer should first build up his *stock*—that will pay him—and only when the pressure on his pasture from stock becomes intolerable should he spend a penny on improving his land.

We did buy five cows, at sales, in addition to the two we had (after little Miranda had died) and we engaged in the laborious task of 'multiple suckling'. Whether this was a good thing to do I do not know—I only know it was very hard work.

We would go along to a local 'mart' and buy calves that were being auctioned. Now these calves were the progeny of dairy herds and the one thing the milk producer does not want is —calves. He wants rid of them! There is a law that he may not take them to mart (a word which we use in this part of Britain instead of market) until they are a week old, but this law is more honoured in the breach than in the observance. Every-body in the know is aware that in practice thousands of little calves are dragged to the mart, week after week, when they are a mere day or two old: they are thrown into the backs of vans, or trailers, or the back-seats of old cars, hauled out and flung like sacks of rubbish into pens where they are jammed in among other, strange calves, so that if one has a disease they all catch it; there they wait, cold, hungry and miserable, until they are auctioned, when they are dragged off again, flung into another car, driven many miles, and then either fed with milk substitute from a bucket, or else put to suck on a 'nurse cow' as ours were. She probably kicks them and butts them, and they pick up all sorts of diseases against which they have no immunity. I had a neighbour who was also rearing calves, or trying to, but on a much larger scale than us. I asked him what his method was. 'My method?' he said. 'I buy them on Monday, put them on antibiotics on Wednesday, and bury them on Friday.'

Calves, like human babies, need the colostrum from their mothers; that is, the stuff that colours and flavours the milk for a few days after calving. This confers immunity on the calf

66

for all the things to which the mother is immune. If you drag a calf away from the mother before he has had a few days of colostrum he has no immunity and is easy prey to scores of diseases. Even if he *has* had a week of his mother's milk he has not acquired immunity from the diseases of his new surroundings. But, of course, if a dairy farmer leaves a calf on its mother for a week he will suffer a considerable loss: that flush of milk during the first week after calving is financially important to him. Therefore very few calves get this protection.

So we had the white scours and the yellow scours and the bloody scours and the stinking scours (scour means diarrhoea). Sally nursed the little animals back to health, taking them off milk and putting them on glucose and water, popping antibiotics into their mouths (yes, there was no other way—it was either that or lose them), keeping them warm, and yet with enough air, being kind to them, trying to make their foster mothers be kind to them, and all the rest of it. Women are certainly far better at looking after sick animals than men. Or perhaps I should say most women than most men. Whatever the current theories on the subject there is no doubt that women are different from men, and much better than men are at many things, and looking after sick calves is one of them. We reared perhaps a hundred calves in that first couple of years and as I remember only one of them died. If other people managed to rear eighty per cent they thought they were doing pretty well.

We looked upon ourselves as organic farmers—and yet there we were putting antibiotics into calves. But there is no doubt that the calves would have died if we hadn't dosed them. Of course the fact is that this method of rearing calves is itself incompatible with organic agricultural philosophy. The calves should never have been taken away from their mothers in the first place. We have reared scores of calves here on their own mothers' milk—calves that were born here and stayed here until we had either sold them, eaten them, or put them into our dairy herd—and we have never had one even seriously sick. It may be objected that if every cow reared her own calves there would be no surplus milk to feed people. The answer to this is that there would—but not quite so much. Modern cows have been bred to yield far more milk than their calves consume, and there is no reason why one should not take as much milk as one needs for oneself and leave enough for the calf. This is, in fact, what we do at Fachongle Isaf now and it works perfectly well. But unrestricted commercial competition rather than straight human greed has forced dairy farmers into wanting every drop of milk they can get, and has obliged other farmers to specialize, as we did, in this horrid trade of dragging little animals away from their mothers and rearing them up artificially—generally on milk substitutes of one kind or another—and if a large proportion of them die in misery, well that must just be regarded as a natural hazard. And until we can get back to true organic agriculture again—an agriculture which is informed with respect for all life, vegetable and animal—we shall have to put up with this kind of cruelty.

As far as other farming matters were concerned, we borrowed a tractor, ploughed up Parc y Banc Isaf and sowed it to barley and oats. We got a neighbour to drill the seed, but thereafter we practised the art of 'broadcasting'—that operation depicted in so many sentimental Victorian Bible illustrations whereby a man walks along the field throwing seed out of a bag or basket that hangs round his neck. It is a fine thing to do—one feels that it is such a generous gesture, giving open-handedly to the Good Earth that it may give back to animals and Man. George Hughes broadcast the first field that we did like this (Parc y Croesffordd) and he taught me how to do it. I have done it ever since but of course I will never be as good as George was. It is a fine feature of our older society here that we have our acknowledged experts who go round the district doing their thing. This is true specialization of the best kind. George Hughes, before he got too old, was the man who broadcast your seed. It is a fine art to look at an irregularly shaped field and at some sacks of seed and thereupon, with no further ado, spread that seed over every inch of that field so that when the crop comes up it is absolutely even, and when you get to the last corner of the field you cast the last handful of the seed on the last few square yards. Not an ounce of seed remains over, not a square yard of field remains unsown. And, as all old farmers will tell you, 'it's when the crop comes up that we shall see how well you've done it!' A field is a canvas upon which the artist cannot

keep painting out and painting in again—he is only allowed one
brush stroke for each area.

Tom Brithdir is *the* man who does all our ridge ploughing
for us. This has to be, for John Greystones is the only man who
owns a ridging plough in our little coterie and John won't allow
anybody (including himself) to use it but Tom. So Tom has to
go round to all of us who grow potatoes on more than a garden
scale and ridge our land for us. I am the only man in our particular little lot who has a rigid-tine cultivator and I often have a job
to lay my hands on it—it is very popular and spends a lot of
its time visiting neighbours. I don't resent the inconvenience of
this at all—I like it, for don't I continually borrow my neighbours' implements? I remember Tom coming to me once and
begging almost apologetically if he could borrow—his—tractor
plough. But this year I lent him my mare and horse-hoe, to go
through his garden with. And there is one contribution I have
been able to make. In this land of rocks I am the only man for
miles who knows how to use—or can get—explosives. There
was a time when I really did get tired of neighbours coming to
me to ask if I could blow up rocks for them, for it meant that I
had to go to the police to get a permit, to the quarry to get the
stuff, and then to the neighbour to do the job. But I have broken
some scores of rocks on my own farm with gelignite and thereby
cleared fields which are now very productive.

These were the top ends of Parc y Croesffordd and Parc Nes
y Ty, which had twenty-three huge rocks on them, each as big
as a bus, and which no J.C.B. could touch. I dug round them
so as to bare as much of the rock as I could (less cushioning
effect like this) and put down heavy 'mud blasts' (these are large
wads of gelignite hammered well down on to the rock and then
covered with wet mud. The gelignite, when it goes off, does
not know that the mud is only a few inches deep—water being
incompressible—and so drives its shock equally down into the
rock); I fused the charges with capped fuses and strolled off to
have coffee. It was then, and not until then, that I noticed the
great fleet of charabancs and cars which were proceeding past
our gate. On making enquiries I discovered that they were
inducting the new Minister at the Baptist Chapel at Caersalem
that very day. Caersalem is a couple of hundred yards from the

field which I was blowing up. I went and spoke to an Elder of
the Church who said that the best time for me to blow the
charges would be during lunch when everybody would be out
of the Chapel and the service would not be disrupted.

Sure enough at lunch time many cars streamed past, going off
towards Newport, where who knows what the many faithful
did with their lunch hours—stayed out of the pubs it is only
to be hoped. I thereupon sent children—some on horses—along
every road leading to the farm with orders to stop every passer-
by until I shouted the all clear. The twenty-three charges were
large ones, for mud-blasting is an inefficient way of using ex-
plosive and the Preseli Bluestone is about the hardest rock in
the world. Sally and I were to light twenty fuses and another
person who shall be nameless was to light the three over the
other side of the field.

I shouted 'cheesa!' which means 'fire' in Kitchen-Kaffir (I
learned my explosives in the copper mines of what is now
Zambia), and Sally and I began to light fuses. We lit our quota
and walked back to the house for safety. You must never run
when lighting fuses—it is bad for your morale. Shattering
explosions began to go off—that lovely hard *crack* that tells the
blaster that his rocks are breaking. As you always must, I counted
the shots. 'Eighteen . . . nineteen . . . twenty . . . twenty-one.'
No less—no more. 'Two haven't gone off,' I said to Sally. 'I
must give them ten clear minutes before I go and see why not.'

By then the faithful were streaming back from—well, not
the pub, but wherever they had been—and there was impatient
hooting. I walked along the row of cars and explained what was
happening. Being Welsh people they were tolerant (we are all
patient with each other's foibles here, maybe because we all
have so many) but it seemed a long ten minutes.

I walked into the field, turned about among the shattered
rocks, and came to two of the three that our helper was to set
off where the fuses had not been lit at all. A scattered box of
matches told the tale. The person had lit one charge—run (that's
where he went wrong) to the next, fumbled, dropped the match
box—and fled.

6   *Social Matters*

When small, our three eldest children went to the primary
school in Newport in the bus every day, and brought friends
back with them. Our house began to be full of children. There
was one family in particular—I will call them the O'Connors
because their father was of Irish extraction—that practically
adopted us—or could it be that we adopted them? There were
ten of them, all crammed in a council house with Mum and
Dad. As each one got to a certain age—about eight I should
guess—he or she began draggling up from the town (it's a good
two miles, and hilly) to 'help' me on the farm. For years I
always had an O'Connor child with me like a sort of squire, or
page. They were without exception splendid and beautiful
children, and extremely intelligent. They were intelligent enough
not to want to be 'academics', and shamelessly *miched*, as they
called it, i.e. stayed away from school. They could learn anything they wanted to learn very easily but anything they did
not want to learn—such as the Date of the Accession to the
Premiership of the Elder Pitt—they just would have no truck
with at all. We had ponies and the O'Connors not so much
learned to ride as just discovered they *could* ride—they seemed
to have been born with the aptitude. A Gypsy horse-dealer
friend of mine, watching little Patrick (I disguise their names
so as not to embarrass them) gallop by, bareback, on a half-
broken pony, said 'You could earn a fortune with that boy.
Real business-boy that is. Real business-boy!' What he meant
was that you could put Patrick on any wild or half-broken
horse and show the horse off to a prospective buyer, who would
then give you a good price for the animal thinking how well
broken it was.

I taught them to sail; I taught them to fish; strictly against
the law I taught them to drive the tractor; I taught them to

drive working horses about the farm; to milk; Sally taught them to make butter and cheese; they helped me kill pigs (no feigned squeamishness with the O'Connor children); and for years in holiday time at least (and often, reprehensibly perhaps, in term time too) it was as though I was a man with four hands —I could always say, when doing a job: 'hold this!' or 'fetch that!' and it was held or fetched. Very often I did not have to say it—a tool or a piece of material just appeared to my hand when I needed it. Mostly the current incumbent O'Connor just didn't bother to go home—he or she would simply move into our household just like our own children.

One of the saddest and most destructive things that our 'technological' society has done is to break completely this natural interaction between child and grown-up. In medieval times the children naturally worked and played among the adults, keeping the latter sane and young-minded, and themselves taking in, with the air they breathed, the skills, learning, and lore of the human world. Now the adults are herded into offices and factories, where the children never go, and the children into huge, ugly, glass-walled, impersonal, loveless 'schools' where they sit out their lives, hunched over desks, being bored to tears by having useless, irrelevant, and very often suspect information stuffed into them.

There is room—and a need—for academics. Possibly one child in twenty—or one in a hundred (what was the proportion two hundred years ago?) might want to be a scholar or a scientist, and should be encouraged to do so—provided, of course, that he or she is not allowed to be completely divorced from the adult world and the world of practical work. But to continue to drive the whole child population into huge buildings like sausage factories, and teach them (as most teachers do) that the only honourable aim in life is to stuff themselves with academic information and beat their peers at exams, and become civil servants or office workers, and that it is somehow shameful to be a worker with one's hands, is to ensure misery for children and disaster for the human race.

Because of very real child exploitation during the Industrial Revolution there has been a revulsion against children doing anything that is useful at all. The summer school holiday is still called the 'Harvest Holiday' in the country, because the original idea of it was that children could help with the harvest. Children now are allowed nowhere near the harvest field. It is against the law for them to ride on a tractor or go anywhere near any machine and everything is done now on the farms by machinery. Of course the law is more honoured in the breach than the observance—I was talking to a country policeman once when a tractor came along the road with children clinging all over it like ants around a dying beetle. The P.C. discreetly withdrew behind a hay stack while the tractor passed so that he should not be seen to be seeing. Of course, in a country of sixty million inhabitants, accidents take place, but they are prevented by trusting to the good sense of responsible individuals —not by passing silly laws. I repeat, laws passed by townspeople for the governance of country people are invariably a mistake. The only saving factor is that, nearly always, we don't have to take any notice of them.

But to get back to this question of children working—because some children worked for sixteen hours a day in the cotton mills it is ridiculous to stop for ever the good practice of children helping their elders, for a few hours a day, at healthy, pleasant and fruitful work. I have found that children *love* work provided they can see the point of it and don't have to do it for too long each day. My little son Dai (now nine) will spend a full day in the harvest field, working as hard as any man, because he *wants* to. He spent just such a day yesterday. Today he is playing with his family of 'trolls' in a hollow tree down by a beautiful stream—but he did not go down to play until he had helped his mother with the morning chores. He would have been very insulted if she had not allowed (indeed, expected) him to. To force children like the O'Connor children to stay at what is to them a prison of a school until they are sixteen, when they have learnt everything they wish to from school by the age of ten, is monstrous. Children so incarcerated are just as deprived as the children of a hundred years ago forced to work sixteen hours a day in the cotton mills. To an academically-minded child secondary school can be fun. To a child such as I was, and such as the O'Connor children were, it is hell on earth—one long ordeal by boredom, and all the time that such

73

children spend hunched over dreary books is time wasted—
time that should be the most vital and important time of a
child's development, when he or she should be learning the
real business of life: the business of producing food, caring for
the land, producing good artifacts, enriching life for all people
on earth, and, in fact, all of life itself. The present school system
is a huge, self-perpetuating, self-enlarging creation of the
National Union of Teachers. It is being run *by* the N.U.T. *for*
the N.U.T. and not for the children, or the world of the future,
at all. We must 'de-school' society (as Professor Illich urges us
to) very urgently otherwise we shall have a whole nation of
clerks and scientists and people on the dole and we shall starve
to death.

Old George Fachongle, when he said (perhaps more satirically
than I gave him credit for)—'Beeros! Beeros!', meaning, as I
mentioned before, that his sons-in-law were men who worked
with ball-point pens and not in dirty boots, was putting his
finger on a great disaster of our age. Give me the men with the
dirty boots, any time: they are the ones who feed us all, in the
last resort.

So, what with our own children, and the O'Connors, and
various other cronies that collected round us, we were never
allowed to become that saddest of all societies—an adult ghetto.
But we had plenty of teenagers and young adults too. Sally
always had her 'Handmaiden'—the title I gave the girls—when
the children were young. Sally wanted to be free to pot, and
could very easily sell enough pots to pay a Handmaiden, and
so she always had one. They just seemed to arrive from nowhere when they were wanted; each one would stay for a year
or two, fall in love, and get married. They were simply part of
the family while they were with us—our eldest daughter, that's
all. But if I acknowledged all their progeny as my grandchildren
I would be like King Solomon himself.

They were all pretty girls, the Handmaidens; and happy and
fun-loving ones too. They had to be, otherwise we wouldn't
have had them. They attracted plenty of admirers as well as
girlfriends of their own age. Thus our house used to have large
gatherings of young people in it—many a time I have counted
eighteen or twenty of us sitting round the big fire in the evening.

And our neighbours, too: the older ones all looked upon Fachongle Isaf as what it was—open house to them, where all were welcome and hospitably treated. The whole idea of growing your own food, baking your own bread, killing your own meat, and brewing your own beer, is so that you *can* be hospitable. My standards of hospitality were different from Sally's, and I know that she often used to wish we had fewer guests, but I had passed my formative years in Africa where everybody, whether black or white, took hospitality completely for granted. I walked down from the Copper Belt to Lusaka once with a man named Jack Smart, both of us out of work and completely bankrupt, in the rainy season when the road was completely closed to motor traffic, and for six weeks we dined every night on sweet potatoes and chicken, never went to bed without a debbie-full of native beer (a debbie was a four-gallon petrol tin), nearly always attended a dance given in our honour, and, if it was raining, always had a hut lent us. That was black Africa, but if you rode up to a white-owned farmhouse, anywhere in Africa, the first thing you heard would be the master's voice bawling: '*Boy! Bring bietjie coffee!*' The unheralded and unexpected guest was to be treated with instant and unquestioning hospitality and you were welcome to stay as long as you liked: in the farmer's house if you were white, in the 'Kaffir compound' if you were black. Having been brought up in this tradition I cannot now go back to the Northern European habit of half-opening the door and saying: 'Hullo. What can I do for you?' making it quite clear, by your tone of voice, that you have no intention of doing anything for the person at your door at all.

We had, and thank God still do have, people from every possible sort of social stratum sitting at our fireside. Often people are pretty incompatible, but I think it is one of the duties of a host to bring them together and try to make them slightly less so. I remember once when a certain county councillor was visiting me—a very respectable man, descendant of a long line of preachers and a pillar of County society. An old truck came down the drive and four Gypsy friends of mine (and I mean Gypsies with a capital G, and not didicois, hedge-mumpers and above all not tinkers) jumped out of it, dragging behind them no less than four cases of bottled ale, and barged into the

75

living-room. They had come from Chester way and were heading for the early potato picking in West Pembrokeshire. I
managed to calm my councillor friend's fairly urgent desire to
say goodbye and we all sat round a big fire, drank the beer and
ate salt bacon and home-made bread; the county councillor
listened with pleasure and amazement to the truly amazing
stories he was being told, we sang and played the mouth organ
and step-danced, and a very good time was had by one and all.
'John,' said this grave councillor when they had gone, 'I am
very grateful to you. I would *never* have been able to get into
that society without your help. And I found them quite
fascinating.'

When we had evenings of predominantly Welsh-speaking
farming neighbours they invariably developed into singing and
if we were lucky the singing could be very fine. Some young
English people brought up on 'Yah! Yah! Yah!', or 'Yeh!
Yeh! Yeh!' cannot 'get into' Welsh singing. The reason is that
they cannot understand the extreme beauty and cleverness of
that truly Welsh art: harmonizing. Rock has its own harmonies
of course—but they are infinitely simple, whereas those of
Welsh singing are infinitely subtle.

All our neighbours can sing, but scattered among us are
some veritable giants of the epiglottis. There were four brothers:
Alwain Owen, one of Newport's two butchers; Mansel, the
Monumental Mason; Noel the Postman, and another, older,
brother who unfortunately went away to earn his living in a far
country, used to come back only seldom, and is now no more.
All these men were fine singers and those who are still with us
still are. Any one of them could have been trained to the very
highest professional standard there is. But it is invidious even
to name names. We have singers galore and magnificent ones
too, and in Welsh there are thousands of good songs. There is
a wealth of good folk songs, buried under puritanism since the
Methodist revolution but being unearthed in these more liberal
days. We always, of course, get down to hymns in the end:
great rolling, thunderous, magnificent hymns that would lift
up the heart of a saint or sinner, deist or atheist, for they are
not hymns to any particular deity, but to the unconquerable
spirit of Man.

The teenagers and young twenty-year-olds were more of a problem, for they knew no songs (they don't even know their own 'Yeh! Yeh! Yeh!' ones further than the first line), they were too self-conscious to dance (unless they got *very* drunk) and some of them were pretty inarticulate. But with no Youth Club in Trefdraeth (a rival gang has always come and smashed it up when there has been one) they had nowhere to go and just loved to come to our house. Well, I hope we did them good for they certainly did us good, and most of them are still close friends. But I can't help thinking that many of these young people would be so much happier and so much more fulfilled if there had not been this unhappy break between the generations, if there was no dole or national assistance, but honest work for all, and if they had not been forced to become failed 'academics' during their boring years at school.

We have a whole generation of disenchanted and alienated young people.

We were cheered up immensely by a splendid person called Horse-drawn (later shortened to Horse) who drove up to our farm one day in a horse-drawn caravan, or *vardo* as Gypsies call it. This young man, the son of a surgeon who was head of an enormous hospital north of London, had built this caravan and headed away from home intending to go to the North of Scotland. His horse had had other ideas, had sometimes gone left when his driver would have had him go right, and Horse, who really didn't care where he went, landed up, purely fortuitously, on our farm instead. He lived for a year or two in his *vardo*, writing poetry, helping on the farm as the fancy took him, and was an enormous asset to our community. He was the first, perhaps, of a new wave of settlers that was to come to our countryside. He wore a beard, long hair, many of the appurtenances that we have now come to know as marks of the Hip generation. He was the first of this movement to impinge on us, and we never found him anything else but delightful; he introduced our children to all sorts of disturbing ideas, which I confess, I feared somewhat when I first began to be aware of them, but find perfectly acceptable now.

There are two wings of the Hippy movement. In one the members are disenchanted with the square world but are perfectly willing to live for ever as parasites on its institutions and labours, drifting from one hippy festival to another, smoking 'pot' grown by, and transported by, the squarest of squares, playing electric guitars produced in huge Japanese factories by sweated labour. Every time they bust a string it is money in the pockets of some establishment millionaire.

The other wing consists of people who are determined to build a world of their own—to free themselves from the square capitalist world—to till the soil and grow their food and create their workshops and artifacts and live by their own honest efforts. Horse-drawn was the first one of these to come to us. He now works a good little farm further inland from here and is a model of hard working self-sufficiency. He married our current Handmaiden, they have a charming little son, and very happy they are too: it delights me to visit them.

Horse-drawn wrote many poems during his stay with us and here, with his permission, is one of them:

opus 104
a party at fachongle isaf
is an event
which attracts all the guests
without the need of invitations
the guests arrive
and so there is a party
and Sally finds hidden bottles of home-made wine
and home brew
and the jug goes round and round
and back to be filled again
and back to go round again
and who doesn't sing is in his grave
and who doesn't laugh was never born
and the kids are trying to be tipsy
and trying not to be tipsy
and being tipsy
and all is like a ceremony to celebrate the joy of the house
and the richness of the house
and there are never enough chairs
which means there are enough people

and the house is alive from the stone flags
to the roof slates
from the beams and timbers to the round welsh stones in the
    walls
and he whose magic draws the fairy guests
plays his melodion to make them sing
to make them dance
to make the children leap like madmen
till they swing from the ceiling bars
and their flying feet endanger lives and pots
and potation spills in welcome libation
and everyone gasps and starts again
with a new song
and Sally sings with the quietest voice you never had trouble
    hearing
and John sings like a drunken pirate
which he would like to be
which he is
and nobody goes away
without feeling they partook in something
which made them something more
than they were before

and when I go back to the caravan
out of the door
the blast of millions and millions and millions
of great flaming screaming stars
leap out of the universe at me
and it seems that the privilege of humanity
is that it is humanity.

Richard Plewes

7 Bread and Other Matters

Fachongle Isaf has now achieved the state of complete self-sufficiency in food with the exception of tea and coffee, and that with a population of about fourteen people all the year round and an average of about twenty-five in the summer, and with many visitors at all times of the year. We now have sixty-two acres of which only forty are workable. But more of all this later.

The point is that when Sally, and our children, and our Handmaiden, and maybe the odd young person or two like Horse-drawn lived here we were still nearly self-supporting, although we did have to buy animal feeding stuffs and we did not grow wheat every year. On such years as we did not grow wheat we would buy flour ready ground at a watermill the other side of Carmarthen. The story of this watermill (and nearly every other watermill in Wales and England) is shocking in the extreme. At a time when the world is running out of oil it pleased our government to set up some monstrous 'water-authority' (a 'water-nanny') which promptly clapped a huge tax on all water 'used' by watermills. Of course such water is not really used at all—it is merely borrowed from the stream for a few seconds while it goes round the waterwheel. But the tax is such that it has caused nearly every surviving watermill in the country to abandon its waterwheel and install either electric power or a diesel engine. 'Whom the gods wish to destroy . . . ' and of course our watermill closed its wheel down too. Anyway, we grow our own wheat now and have done for some time.

To take some wheat seed out into a field and sow it and eventually make a loaf of bread from the wheat thus grown is not as simple as it seems. You not only have to grow it, you have to harvest it, store it, thresh it, winnow it, store the resulting grain, grind it, and bake it. Cobbett was thinking of all this when he inveighed, as only he could, against the potato—which he called 'the lazy root'. Cobbett's belief was that wheat, made into bread, was not only the best food for sustaining a high civilization, but also that it was the cause of civilization itself, simply because it was so difficult, and took such a degree of organization, to produce. He imagined potato-eaters, particularly what were to him the benighted Irish, going out into the fields and scrabbling in the earth for potatoes, which they then proceeded to eat raw without even wiping the dirt off, or at the very most boiling them, whereas your bread-eater has to know all about the complex processes of turning wheat into bread, and is forced into habits of discipline and industry in order to stay alive.

Possibly there is something in this. Certainly it was the millwrights, who showed such astonishing ingenuity over the centuries developing water and windmills to grind corn, who led the way into the Industrial Revolution. They were the only class of people who understood about such things as applied power, gearing, mechanical advantage, and all the rest of it, and if the people of Northern Europe had been potato-eaters and not wheat-eaters, there would have been no millwrights and probably no Industrial Revolution. Which might, of course, have been a very good thing.

Anyway, we have harvested wheat here by sickle, by scythe, with a binder (a machine which both cuts and binds up corn into sheaves), a combine harvester. We have had it threshed in the field by combine harvester, or in the barn in the winter with a stationary combine harvester, we have threshed it by flail, and by bashing it over the back of a chair. The latter method sounds ridiculous, but it is surprising how quickly you can knock out a hundredweight like this—and after all a small family does not require many hundredweight a year to live on. We have winnowed it (blown the chaff away from the grain) either in a combine harvester (in the past I have done it with a hand-turned winnowing machine) or more often by flinging it up over a tarpaulin on a windy day. The grain falls in a nice clean heap on the tarpaulin and the chaff blows away. This is a very pleasant, amusing and surprisingly quick way of doing it. Grinding we have done with a small mill driven by a tractor, in various hand-turned coffee grinders, and in hand-turned grain mills, like the Atlas, which we have now.

I am not suggesting that the world should go forward (you can never 'go back'—time moves forward and so nobody can ever go *back*) to threshing wheat with the flail and winnowing it in the wind. But I do think that all of us who live in areas in which wheat can be grown should go forward to growing wheat on farms in our own areas (instead of carting it halfway round the world), cutting and tying it with the binder which has many advantages over the combine harvester (for example, it allows the grain to mature and dry naturally in the stook and the stack and thus make better bread), grind it in the village mill, which would thus give pleasant and useful work to the villagers, and bake it in the village bakehouse if we do not, indeed, bake it ourselves. There is just nothing in the world to beat good Welsh or English wheat (it does not have to be 'hard'—'hardness' in wheat simply means that the flour will contain more water and gas and thus the baker can sell water and holes for the same price as good bread) fairly coarsely ground, with nothing taken out, nothing added, and baked properly with yeast in an oven of 450°F. The result is absolutely superb bread and, once you have got used to it, so superior to the wrapped sliced pap of the steamed-'bread' factories that you can never go back to that stuff. If the kind of bread I have described forms a good part of a person's diet from childhood on, that person will never need to go to the dentist and all such nonsense as the fluoridation of water supplies will be superfluous.

But this matter of bread may be taken as a model for nearly every other agricultural and industrial activity. For every villager to grow wheat except huge specialist wheat farmers in East Anglia and Canada, and for this wheat to be ground only in a few enormous mills, and the resulting flour baked in a few enormous factories (it is wrong to call them bakeries—they do not bake the bread, they steam it) is far too far along the road to specialization. For good professional family farms in every area of the British Isles in which wheat can reasonably be grown to grow the wheat for their locality, for this to be ground in the village mill (preferably a mill driven by a non-polluting and non-extractive form of power such as wind or water) and baked in the village mill—that is just the right distance along the road to specialization.

My reasons for this assertion are as follows.

For everyone to grow wheat in his backyard is not a good idea because the sparrows would simply eat too much of the crop, everyone would have to spend too much time over this one small item of growing bread, and the resulting bread, in many instances, probably wouldn't be very good. That is why I say that such a practice is not far enough along the road to specialization.

For nobody but a few huge farmers in certain very favourable areas to grow wheat, for it to be ground in a few huge mills and steamed in a few huge bread factories is bad for the following reasons:

1. It causes monoculture—the growing of only one, or a limited number, of kinds of crops on the land. This is bad farming, vitiating the soil and ultimately producing vitiated crops. And it not only causes monoculture in the countries which specialize in wheat—it also causes it in other countries: e.g. in my particular country, because it prevents farmers from growing wheat and forces them to practise a grass-and-cow monoculture which is just as damaging, in its way, as wheat monoculture. Successful monoculture is always entirely dependent on large inputs of fuel and chemicals.

2. It draws more people to the big cities where the huge mills and bread factories are. This is bad because there are a lot of disguised disadvantages. People are not so happy or so healthy in big cities as they are in small villages. The overall crime bill of the country is higher because the cities are too big, and so is the overall health bill including the mental health bill. In every way it is bad for people to be drawn into the big cities or for these cities to get bigger.

3. It is bad for the villages, because it destroys two of the economic props of village life: the mill and the bakery. It weakens the village both economically and socially.

4. It causes more traffic on the roads (to say nothing of more shipping on the seas and congestion in ports). More traffic on the roads means that more roads have to be built, thus taking up more land that should be producing food, creating more air and noise pollution, causing more people to get injured and killed on the roads, more towns and villages to become un-

endurable because of the weight of traffic going through them. Unfortunately the people who *should* bear the costs of these disadvantages never do—they get off Scot-free. For example, the owners of the great fleets of wrapped-pap vans that carry the surrogate 'bread' around, often for hundreds of miles from where it was processed, do not have to pay for the damage this traffic causes to the countryside that it goes through, nor for the hospitalization of people who get knocked down, nor for the physical and mental health bills that are increased by noise, fumes and congestion.

Now for my third alternative: for good professional family farms to grow wheat in every district in which wheat can reasonably be grown, and for this wheat to be ground in the village mill and baked in the village bakery. This is far and away the best alternative for the following reasons:

1. It tends to encourage mixed farming as opposed to monoculture, because the same principle that applies to wheat will apply to other things: farms will tend to produce a little of everything that is needed by the people in the immediate district. This is good because it makes for better husbandry practice than monoculture: the more variety of both crops and stock that is kept on the land the more fertile that land will be, for everything takes something different out of the land and puts something different back into it.

2. It is good because such farming employs more people on the land: the insane drive for more and more 'labour-saving' farming has depopulated the countryside and filled the cities with idlers and wasters who are doing no good to themselves or anybody else. They would be far better employed back in the country, where their ancestors came from, tilling the soil.

3. It makes for a more diverse and interesting countryside than monoculture. It is good to see a great variety of crops and stock about one. It is good to know the name of the farmer who grew the wheat one eats in one's bread, the name of the miller who ground it, and the baker who baked it.

4. Transport is saved, and with it the vast amount of fuel that is needed to transport, for example, wheat from Winnipeg to the coast, by sea to a British port, by road to a mill, by more road transport to a distant bread factory, and from the factory

to the distant customer. Much of the 'bread' eaten in my part of the world was steamed in Cardiff, a hundred miles away.

5. It allows of a farming and milling industry that is less dependent on dwindling stocks of fossil fuel. Mixed agriculture docs not require the enormous inputs of fuel-derived fertilizers and chemicals apart from the saving of fuel that comes from less transport.

6. It strengthens and improves local life. The reason why our villages are dull and lack social cohesion now is that so many of the traditional small village industries have died and home-made products have been replaced by imports from faraway cities, often in faraway countries. The death of the village mill was a blow to the village, just as were the deaths of the village blacksmith, harness-maker, carpenter, wheelwright, cobbler, tailor, and all the others, culminating, in so many of our villages (including my own) in the demise of the school. When the school goes the village dies, and there is an end of it.

7. You get better bread.

Now I don't think it's particularly appropriate for me to have to go through all the complex processes of growing wheat, processing it, and baking in order to get bread. But this is the only way in which I can be sure of getting what I want for myself and my children: good honest wholemeal bread grown from wheat that has not been dragged halfway round the world. I would far prefer to be able to sell my wheat to a miller that I knew and buy my bread from a baker whom I knew and not have to go to all that trouble myself. But until I can do this (and the answer to the question of whether it will ever happen again is that we must *make* it happen) I will go to the trouble of making my own bread from my own wheat.

And for bread read practically every other foodstuff, or arti-fact, that human beings need. We should strike, ourselves, the right stage along the road of specialization in everything, and not allow this choice to be left to the 'blind workings of the market'. We are not blind. Pappy, steamed bread made in a factory a hundred miles away, from wheat ground another hundred miles away, and grown three thousand miles away, may be assumed to be cheaper than the bread we bake right here at Fachongle from wheat we grow ourselves. Astonishingly

85

enough it isn't, and if you buy wheat from a farmer and grind it yourself and bake your own bread in an electric cooker, and keep careful accounts, you will find that you are getting very cheap bread. But even if it *were* cheaper it still would not be *better*: better for our souls, our bodies, our happiness, and the peace, health and beauty of our countryside. But do have that oven at least 400°F and allow the dough to 'prove' (rise) twice.

Vegetables, of course, are no problem on a farm any more than if you live in a house with a suburban garden. You just grow them and eat them, and that is all. We explored very fully the business of storing them, but in the southern British climate you really do not need to store vegetables much: you can have a year-round succession of fresh green things out of the garden without going to a lot of trouble deep-freezing and the rest of it. We have a deep-freeze but hardly ever use it for vegetables. I like to come fresh to peas in June—and not with a palate jaded with eating frozen peas all winter through. This I must admit though: Sally's vegetable garden ('The Round Garden') was always much better than mine ('The Long Garden'). This was because she is a more careful gardener than I am, more energetic than I am, and at home far more often than I am. I was only able to keep the Long Garden going at all by using the horse to drag a cultivator up and down between the rows, and for ploughing. And sometimes, alas, it really did get neglected. But in a dozen years I don't remember us ever being short of a green vegetable—although we often did have to get down to eating curly kale, and rather too much spinach for my liking.

Meat we had in plenty, partly due to the deep-freeze. Most years we killed an ox, or at least a bull calf or two, and cut this up and froze most of it. Sheep were easier: in the winter you can kill and eat a sheep without freezing it if you are a large family and tend to give some of the meat away to neighbours. The old neighbourly tradition of each farmer taking it in turns to kill an animal and share the meat out among neighbours, was killed by meat rationing in two world wars, and the village butchers now no longer kill local meat: everything has to go to a faraway slaughterhouse (the demise of the village slaughterhouse was another dire blow to village life—besides being much unpleasanter for the animals, which now have to travel miles crammed into the backs of lorries to reach their resting place), and the chill of the deep-freeze has taken the place of the warmth of neighbourly relations. There is still a little unofficial to-ing and fro-ing of joints of meat between farmers but it no longer happens in a sufficiently consistent way.

As for ham and bacon, we fattened and killed three pigs a year and were never for long without salted and smoked pig-meat. Home-cured bacon is superb—*but* you have to know how to use it. Being saltier than shop bacon it has to be soaked before being fried, for the requisite period, and anyway is better boiled and eaten cold, which is the way the farmers used to eat it in the old days. Like that, with mustard and a boiled egg it is superb.

Fruit we did not do too well with, excepting raspberries and blackcurrants which we have had in plenty. Blackcurrants in particular we have bottled, jammed, jellied and wined in great store. We planted pears and apples as soon as we got here but the trees are only just beginning to bear in any quantity and now, as I shall relate, our community has grown so much that the fruit is nowhere near enough for us. Apples and oranges have been two of the things that we have felt it necessary to buy. Blackberries, it is true, have never failed us, and we have always preserved them in great quantity. Most years hazel nuts were there for the picking, and, put down in dry salt in their shells, will last until hazel nuts come again.

Fish—well, there are plenty of them in the sea and all you have to do is go and *catch* them. To do this you need a boat.

8   Of Fish and the Sea

Fortunately we had a boat.

But she was in Suffolk, three hundred and fifty miles away. She was a twenty-foot long open 'coble', a class of boat traditional to Northumberland and the coast of Yorkshire as far south as Flamborough Head. These boats were evolved (no coble has ever been *designed*) to operate off open beaches, for the coast from which they fish has few harbours. They are therefore a very distinctive design. They have high narrow bows and a deep forefoot, but halfway back along their length they undergo a most extraordinary transformation. From being deep and narrow-gutted they open out, flatten, and become shallow-draughted and quite flat-bottomed. The deep sharp keep of the fore section gives way to two 'draughts', as coblemen call them, which are skegs of wood, or side-keels, shod with iron. The deep forefoot, or forekeel, is shod with iron too.

Now these boats are launched into the sea head-first, so that their sharp high bows are first to meet the breakers while their flat arses slide comfortably over the sand. Their crews row them to deep enough water then ship the heavy, very long slab of rudder that hangs down from three to five feet below the waterline depending on the size of the coble. In sail and oar days the tall dipping lugsail was then set and the boat would sail away out to sea.

When she came back again (and by that time of course an on-shore gale might have blown up, in which case it was just too bad, for there was no harbour) she would sail straight towards the beach; just before the rudder touched bottom (or after it—the rake of the transom being such that the rudder leaps out of its pintles at the slightest touch of the sand) the boat would be swung right round to face the sea, the rudder hauled aboard, oars got out, and the coble backed to land. Thus her flat hindquarters took the ground first and kept her upright while the sharp high bows met and split the waves. I have beached my coble in surf that would have pitch-poled any other boat and left her upside down with me inside her.

It was then that helpers on the beach hove the coble up on to a two-wheeled trolley, and horses in the old days and a tractor now hauled, or haul, the coble up to safety, catch, crew and all.

I had first seen cobles at Filey, when I watched the entire fleet run home before the biggish sea, loaded deep with cod from long-lining, swing round and run on to their trolleys to be hauled up to the Coble Landing by tractors. They had to come in one at a time, so as to give the shore crew time to handle them, and the others circled round outside the breakers waiting (impatiently one imagined, for the wind—and sea—were getting up by the minute) for their turn. They all had powerful engines, of course—the sailing days went long ago.

When I first saw the cobles I knew I had to have one, willy-nilly, and so when I eventually did get one built I named her *Willynilly*, and *Willynilly* she is to this day. She was built by Harrison Brothers of Amble, Northumberland, and when I went to fetch her practically the entire population of the little port tried to persuade me to take her away by land and not to sail her. 'Only a cobleman can sail a coble,' they said. 'Ye'll never handle yon lugsail—ye've got to be born te it. Mony's the coble that's been lost at sea,' they said, 'but none yet has been lost coming to the beach. For a coble's boat and harbour in one.' Well, I've had some hairy moments coming to the beach in mine, but we're both still alive.

I sailed away from Amble on a fine sunny day. I got a tow out of the harbour, cast off outside, and proceeded, for the first time in my life, to try to set a dipping lugsail. Like many primitive things the dipping lug is unbelievably complicated: the simplest sail in the world is the bermudan—the latest thing. The whole population of Amble had turned out to see me go and I could just imagine the price being offered by amateur bookies on whether I should reach my home alive. It shot to prodigious heights as I tried to set that sail upside down, inside out, back to front, around my neck, around me like a shroud, and finally the right way up. And away we sailed. We sailed several hundred miles to Orford in Suffolk, along a coast with very few harbours, and on the whole we went very well.

Then, for good measure, a boy named Mogador and I sailed to the Kiel Canal the next year, and Sally and Jane flew out to join us at Kiel and we sailed round the southern islands of Denmark and over to Sweden as well. So if only a cobleman can sail a coble I reckon I can call myself a cobleman, and, come to think of it, I don't think many professional coblemen of today could *sail* a coble at all, as modern cobles are all motorized.

But there I was, in Pembrokeshire, separated by three hundred and fifty miles of dry land from my coble, and I wanted to go fishing. Bring her by road, several people said. Well, I don't think boats are meant to sail by road and I think it's a pretty poor way of getting a vessel about.

Was it all dry land though? Well no, it wasn't. There are rivers—there are canals. England is networked with waterways, and I thought it would be fun to bring the coble across country. A friend wanted to come with me—in fact he decided to make a film about the voyage.

I drove over to Orford in the Fish Van to get the boat ready. I had seen neither Orford nor *Willynilly* for three years. It was a strange experience going back to our old home, the Broom, after all that time. As I drove through the tiny town of Orford I saw the old houses, the old faces, but didn't stop to talk to anybody. Along the lonely Gedgrave Road, turn off along the sandy track, open the first Forestry Commission gate—and I was immediately struck by the fact that everything looked different: of course the pines had grown several feet since I had last seen them. I had watched those trees grow from saplings, over eight years.

When I came to the Broom itself—it was two gamekeepers' cottages knocked into one in the most remote place possible, with marshes stretching out to an estuary on one side of it and pine woods on the other—I got an even bigger shock.

We had handed the tenancy over, as it were, to two good old friends, who we thought were going to retire there but who didn't because Bill died. His widow used it simply as a holiday cottage. Oh, it was much *tidier*. The old shacky buildings that had been so invaluable to us—where we had milked our cow, stabled our horse, killed our pigs, smoked our bacon—they had all been pulled down and no trace was left of them. Except for the bunch of fruit trees at the top of the drive all the cordon trees, fig trees, our ninety outdoor vines, our various gardens, and the fences round them that kept animals and birds in or out—our 'Goose Bit', 'The Hill', the 'House Garden'—all was an even, closely-mown, lawn of grass. Nothing grew there at all that you could eat, and even the grass was not grown to eat—it was shaved off once a week by a paid man from the town with a motor mower and the good grass thrown away to rot. The place was simply part of urban or suburban England, where Food is something that comes from the supermarkets, and Land is something to play tennis on, or golf, or to sit around in deck chairs and have tea on, or else, in extreme cases, for jolly country folk to ride tractors about on—but a decent distance away.

I am not in any way criticizing Bill's widow, who was then and always has been kindness itself to me. *She* had no other recourse. She couldn't possibly live there, because she was forced to earn a living, and that in Southend-on-Sea. And in her circumstances she did the very best that she could by getting somebody to plough the whole place flat, raze the out-buildings, and put it all down to grass which could then be kept tidy by a weekly run-over with the motor mower. There was nothing else she could have done with it: if she had left it as Sally and I had left it, on that last journey with the Whale, it would have tumbled down to weeds and rubbish and become an eyesore and a nuisance to everybody about.

But to me, it was a shock. I left the van, walked through the surviving apple and pear trees at the top and noticed that they were now coming into full bearing. *We* never got much benefit from them, but as I looked at them I remembered Sally and me sweating as we carried farmyard manure in a tin bath between us, because we had no wheelbarrow when we had planted them eleven years before.

I walked about the place and became unbearably sad. Wherever I went, wherever I looked, memories came back on me.

Now truth to tell, Sally's and my marriage, which had been so blissfully happy at the Broom, was under strain. We had been under great stress in Wales. We were carrying too big a burden of debt, were having to work and worry far too hard, I was having to go away far too often and for too long in order to make money, generally by making television films or radio programmes, to try, vainly, to pay off our debts. Sally, left alone to carry on the work of what was to us a big farm, and look after the kids, and make as many of her beautiful pots as she could so as to add to our meagre income, resented my absences, and although she knew in her mind that I had to go she could never believe it in her heart. And lest anyone should say 'But you were perfectly ready to go *yachting*', I hasten to add that I was getting very well paid for it—for we were making a film. I was doing it for the money.

This feeling that all was not well with us had been unconsciously with me up to then, but as I walked around that shaven land and remembered: 'That's where the gander attacked my little Kate' or 'That's where we cut the elder tree down to build a wood-fired kiln for Sally which never got built' and a thousand other things, all of them happy memories though most of them about hard work, a feeling of unhappiness came over me that was well-nigh unbearable. And it was so lonely. I have been alone perhaps more than most people during my life (particularly if living with primitive tribesmen who have no common language with one can be considered being alone) but I had never, up until then, felt *lonely*. I took a quick look in the house—all clean whitewash, tasteful and (very good) antiques—all—all—strange and different, lonely and cold. And I fled to The Jolly Sailor, down by Orford Quay, and drank a lot of beer.

Willynilly was still there, miraculously, lying to two anchors as I had left her three years before, waiting patiently for me, and that cheered me up.

I had to go back to the Broom to sleep (indeed I refused to give in to what I thought irrational feelings), and I slept with ghosts. I woke up in the morning with them too. This was the room where the midwife and I had sat up night after night for a week, drinking tea until it came out of our ears, waiting for

Anne to be born. And again waiting for Kate to be born. That was the room where I wrote *The Fat of the Land* and a hundred radio programmes to keep the wolf from the door. These were the rooms where we had lived, and loved, and had parties, and enjoyed endless friends, and got drunk, and sung, and brought up a happy little family. But I had the feeling that some good must come of this ordeal; some strengthening of the character if I resisted the ghosts and refused to flee from them.

During the days, for a week, I scraped *Willynilly*, painted her, fitted her out for the voyage, ran into Woodbridge to get shackles, or rope, or a thermos flask, or this or that. The people at The Jolly Sailor got all excited about the coming voyage— as much as if I had been setting out for the Antipodes. I caught the fever and began to have the same feeling. 'I can't see what all the fuss's about,' grumbled one habitué. 'Damn it, he's only going to Pontypool.' He obviously thought I was only going to Newport, Monmouthshire, instead of that far further-flung Newport, *Pembrokeshire*. I felt aggrieved for a moment that anyone could think other than that I was about to make one of the great voyages of history—and then suddenly thought of my impending ditch-crawling expedition and roared with laughter.

A small Cockney boy cycled up one day, when I was painting away, and fell instantly and hopelessly in love with *Willynilly*. She is beautiful. To the discerning nautical eye there is something exceedingly beautiful about a coble, as indeed there is about any vessel evolved over millennia for particularly hard and exacting use. But for a little London Jewish boy it was surprising: he had hardly seen a boat before. He was down for a fortnight on a farm holiday.

He asked shyly if he could help me. Right on, I said, and thereafter, day after day, he was at the boat to greet me in the morning, scraping and painting away quite as well as I did (*and* he went on doing it when I disappeared, as I did from time to time, into the pub), ever ready to leap on his bicycle and speed off for this or that, and when I was there, and often when I wasn't, there he was, faithfully working on the boat.

I knew the question he wanted to ask. And, if he had asked it, I would not have been able to say *no*, even though I knew that *no* was the only possible answer. There is barely room for two to sleep anyway on *Willynilly's* uncompromising bottom boards. But, fortunately for me and my ship-mate to be, he said to me one day, with tears rolling out of his eyes: 'Me Mum says I mustn't even ask if I can come. I've got to go back to school next week.' I found something very important to look at over the other side of the estuary.

On the day we sailed he was down there to see us off, on his bicycle, and at the last minute and very shyly he pulled half a fallow-deer antler out of his knapsack and handed it to me. 'I found this in the forest,' he said. 'I wanted it—but will you take it—for *Willynilly*—for luck.' Well, I've still got it, and part with it I never will.

Dickie, the boy who used to come down to the Broom year after year in his spare time from school, and who was now a master carpenter having served his time, brought a fine clean balk of seasoned ash, and fitted it skilfully into *Willynilly*, athwartships on top of the after 'thoft' (thoft is coblese for 'thwart', which is nautical for seat) so that the end of the beam protruded out over the starboard quarter. *Willynilly* had never been defiled by an engine: her propulsion had been solely by sail and oar, but to go through canals we had to have one, and a firm of outboard manufacturers had lent us a large and powerful one for this voyage: a twenty horsepower 'Johnson', and excellent it was too. But we could not hang it over the stern in the usual way, cobles being such a funny shape, so we compromised by hanging it on the end of this beam that Dickie so skilfully put in place.

The day came and away we sailed.

Willynilly seems to have a peculiar propensity of arriving at places at very extraordinary times. When I had sailed her up (we East Coasters say 'Up South' and 'Down North'—that's the way the tide runs) from Northumberland I had sailed into Whitby, after a spanking sail on a sparkling day and a fresh breeze of wind, in company with a coal miner who had joined me at Seaham Harbour for the ride, to find that Whitby Harbour was absolutely packed and lined with people: people crowded on every possible horizontal surface of the town; on roofs and pieces of masonry and hanging on cranes and on boat decks —everywhere. Colourful, gaily-clad holiday people. And plenty of yachts and small boats—every one of them dressed fore and aft with flags and bunting. After the very rough and lonely sea outside—we had seen not a craft of any sort nor a sign of mankind all day—it was fantastic to sail straight into this absurdly animated scene.

'Oh, it's Whitby Regatta!' said Harry Horton, my collier friend. 'They've no put this on specially for us!'

Well, when we sailed up the Thames, and got near Tower Bridge, we suddenly found ourselves part of a fantastic procession of boats again—large boats though, not little open boats like *Willynilly*: huge lighters, barges, river steamers, tugs and all of them tricked out in the most fantastic way—one dressed as a huge sea serpent a hundred yards long, another as a Viking longship, another advertising somebody's whisky, another with a jazz band on it and all the rest of it. And the shore—and all the bridges—were packed tight with excited people.

'What the hell's happening?' we asked each other. Coming in from the grey and lonely sea it was traumatic. Suddenly, while shooting under a bridge hole, a piece of drift wood (of which the filthy river was full) hit our prop and bust the cotter pin. The engine roared in vain—we were spinning round and round and being carried helplessly by the flood tide.

'Get out the oars!' I shouted, but at that moment a police launch came up, threw us a rope, hauled us out of harm's way—into shallow water on the south side—and we dropped anchor.

'What the hell's happening?' we asked.

'Don't you really know? Don't you read the papers?' they said.

'Well—no,' I told them.

'This is a water procession being held in commemoration of the Great Fire of London,' said a policeman.

We pulled ashore and tied up to the high wall. I climbed a ladder and poked my head over the top. The top of the wall was crowded with happy Cockneys. They looked at me amazed—they couldn't have seen our boat below and I surprised them by apparently climbing up out of the river.

'Here's old Father Neptune!' said one, and he thrust a bottle of beer in my hand.

My shipmate went home to his wife, I pulled out again and

anchored, in the dark now after the hullabaloo was over and the firework display had looked like causing the *second* Great Fire of London, and flopped down in the bottom of the boat, in a blanket, and went to sleep. The tide was ebbing then—old Thames was rushing away out to sea.

At three in the morning I was aware that the tide had turned. No sailor used to sailing in tidal waters could ever sleep so soundly that he would not be aware of that event. I got up, pushed an oar under a thoft so it stuck up in the air at an angle, lit the hurricane lamp and hung it on the end of the oar, hauled up my anchor, and, using the other oar to scull over the stern with, just to steer, I let the young flood take me up under the bridges of London.

We were swept right up through the great city, *Willynilly* and I, under bridge after bridge, the skyline of the riverside sharp against the sky—the stars dimmed by the loom of London's lights. London never *quite* sleeps of course, there is always the faint hum of traffic as a background noise, but somehow I could almost feel the *weight* of those millions of sleeping humans around me; there was a moon, and the whole experience was very beautiful. By breakfast time I was safely tied up at Teddington. My shipmate arrived and made me go all the way back to Westminster because he wanted to film the boat going past the Houses of Parliament. In the event the film we made wasn't much good and was never used.

To cut a lot of ditch-crawling short we sailed up the Thames to Oxford, went by canal to Worcester, into the Severn, down to the Bristol Channel, round South Wales, through Jack Sound and Ramsey Sound, where we spent three days on Ramsey Island with a friend of mine who was the last farming tenant there before that fertile and beautiful island was taken out of food production and given over to the bird watchers. There are fewer birds there now than there were then. And so we reached home.

We've caught thousands of fish in *Willynilly*—almost all of them mackerel. I used to load up the kids in the mackerel season, sail round Dinas Head, catch a few dozen on the way, land at Pwll Gwaelod, the kids would pick up driftwood and make a fire to roast the mackerel, go swimming (while I disappeared inside The Sailor's Safety for a pint), we would eat the mackerel which were absolutely delicious, and sail home catching enough on the way for breakfast next morning.

But after a few such excursions, the day would come when we would really get in among them, hard. And on that day we would catch three or four hundred fish in a few hours. Then it was back to the house, head and gut (we don't head and gut at sea because we like these offal for the pigs), salt them down in a barrel, and our year's supply of salt fish is assured.

One year we thought was going to be a disaster. All we mackerellers went out day after day but nobody could catch in any quantity. Twenty, thirty—just enough to keep us in fresh fish to eat and nothing to spare for the salt barrel. And the trouble was that I was writing, in those days, a series of guide books to the coasts of England. The only coast I had never *sailed* (although by then I had walked every yard of coast from the Scottish-Northumberland border to Bristol) was the coast of the South West. So I had to go and sail it in *Willynilly*, because I will not write about anything I have not experienced.

I was sailing the next day, along with a friend of mine who had just sort of dropped in from nowhere and whose name was Kipper. He made me, beautifully, a new sail out of Number Two Flat—the stuff Nelson used for his main courses. It was, and is, a superb sail but heavy enough for a boat a hundred times *Willynilly*'s size. 'I'll make one more attempt to get the salting mackerel,' I told Sally. Kipper and I went forth and came back with, I think, two fish.

'All right—we'll just have to make do without them,' said Sally. But by then a year with no salt mackerel seemed a penance to me.

We set out next day, and ultimately cruised the coast from Bristol to Lyme Regis; *Willynilly*, besides having sailed round Flamborough Head, and through the Store Baelt, has sailed round Land's End. We sailed away that first day from Trefdraeth, with a gentle fair wind, lazily round Dinas Island, crossed Fishguard Bay, and, also lazily, when we got off Stumble Head, I dropped a line overboard. A mackerel line with feathers, and eight hooks. In seconds I pulled in eight mackerel.

Quickly I flung the boat tent down amidships, between two

thofts, to make a kind of dry pool out of it. By the time I had done this I had another eight fish on my line.

Slowly we stood in towards the tiny harbour of Porth Gain, Kipper steering, and sail just pulling, and frantically I hauled in fish. When we got off the harbour we downed sail, anchored, and started heading and gutting. There were three hundred and eighty fish.

We went ashore to The Cutter Inn, and the *second* thing I did after entering the pub was to telephone Sally.

'Sally—bring the car—and a basket. We've got the winter mackerel.'

It was by then ten o'clock.

'Oh—does that mean I've got to go home and gut them all tonight?' she said after her first surprise.

'Oh, it won't take you long,' I said.

'Well—I suppose we need them,' said Sally.

She duly turned up, with car and basket, by which time Kipper and I, and two good friends who live at Porth Gain (John and Sheila Knapp-Fisher, both fine painters) had downed many pints of beer. And of course, when Sally saw the fish all headed and gutted and lying there like little silver darlings, she was beside herself.

We sailed next day (I think we hit our sleeping bags at three in the morning and caught the tide at six) and the following night were lolloping about in practically no wind and a dense fog—somewhere in the approaches to the Bristol Channel. All night we heard a mournful moaning—of a fog-horn of enormous power and penetration. It seemed very near us. Now we didn't have a chart of that part of the ocean and I wondered constantly what this fog-horn could be.

Dawn broke to reveal an extra-large red lightship looming up out of the disappearing fog. She had *ST GOWAN* painted on her side in huge letters. We pulled alongside. The flood tide was done—we would have six hours to ebb dead against us, for we wished to get to Bristol, and there was no wind. (*Willynilly* had by then divested herself of the indignity of an engine.) 'We'll hang on here until she swings flood,' I said.

By then all the lightship crew—seven of them—were leaning over the side looking at us.

'Come aboard!' they said, and lowered a companion ladder. Up it we climbed.

We met the Captain. 'Can I have a look at your chart?' I asked him. 'I don't know where I am.'

'Don't know where you are!' he said in a broad Suffolk accent. 'And haven't got a chart! You damned yachties have no right to drift about the ocean in a cockleshell with no chart and not knowing where you are. No. I'll not show you my chart—I won't take the responsibility. You can stay on here until she swings and then off you go and if anything happens to you it's not my fault.'

'What part of Suffolk do you come from, sir?' I asked him.

'Suffolk? Are you a Suffolk man, then? The last lightship I had was the Cork . . . ' And before I knew it he said—yes we could look at his charts, as many as we liked, and would we like to go on a tour of inspection of the ship with him? We would, and did, and by the time we sailed away, six hours afterwards, we knew the life story of every single member of the crew.

The St. Gowan Lightship is stationed off St. Govan's Point, in Pembrokeshire. At St. Govan's Point there is an ancient chapel, halfway down a steep cliff, which marks the cell of the saint. He landed there from Ireland in heathen times, was chased by the locals, and hid in a crevice of the rock which closed around him, and was saved. I have written a poem about him—and his lightship. Is he the only saint to have had a lightship named after him?

SAINT GOVAN

What shall we make of this God-haunted mystic
This wild Celtic coenobite—Christ-craving fellow?
Fled he from foemen the rock rose round him
Saved him from sword-bite—preserved him for preaching
Did his best he, no doubt, for the time that he lived in
And lest that we sneer or suspect superstition
Let us wonder—have *we* got the keys of the kingdom?
Was he wrecked there or flung there—evangelical sailor
Driven to land where the wave foams on cliff-foot?
Crushed the man's curragh he scrambled a stranger

Up tumbled boulders—the foam-riven cliff-way
Was he met there by Heathen? Was he right? Were they right?
Were they right to resist his pacific religion
That was yet to kill millions? Then did miracle make them
Accept his proposals—his tale of salvation?
Hard pressed by foemen he hid in a crevice
And the hole is still there—you can see it—I've seen it,
Got in it. And wish and your wish will be granted
Mine wasn't. But then are our wishes all lawful?
And built of the boulders that jumble the cliff face
His chapel. Still standing. Still the shrine of Saint Govan.
For twelve hundred years has he owned it his spirit
For twelve hundred years Govan's looked on the Ocean
The wild western ocean a highway to Christians
Saint Dewi—Saint Padraig—they made it their mainroad.
Did a bright light shine forth from this humble Saint Govan
A light shining strong on this ocean of darkness?

Seven miles out from Saint Govan's Point in Pembrokeshire
A lightship swings to two enormous anchors
With two more lashed on deck in case the first ones
Come home as sailors say—that's drag—in tempest.
When things get bad down go the lot—and chain
In scores of tons goes after. Her bows uprisen
Crash down in turmoil. Seas we can't imagine
Come riding in from out the far Atlantic.
This furthest flung of all our country's lightships
Is named *SAINT GOWAN. GOWAN* for *SAINT GOVAN.*
White letters six foot high on red sides blazoned.
Far flings her light beam. Seen eleven miles
My chart says. And fog-horn louder far than any preacher
Christian or Pagan. The crew get special money
And God they earn it—when that thing's agroaning
Shaking the ship—killing all hope of slumber
For some. Some say it's when it *stops* they waken
From fog-horn-riven dreams by silence shaken.
And when, fog-shuttered, from furthest reach of Ocean
The watching sailor filled with high elation
Because his homeward voyage is near completion

Hears the first hint of dismal fog-horn moaning
Or, on a clear night, sees the beam a-winking
'That's the old lightship!' shouts he to his watch-mates
'Saint Govan preaching to the gulls and gannets!
'By God! I'll soon be home and in the arms of Nancy!'
Oh noble lightship—drift not from thy station
And let no Whitby Synod dim thy beacon!

9 *Earning the Other Sort of Bread*

There are around us, here in Pembrokeshire, plenty of crackpots like ourselves. That is, plenty of 'self-sufficiency freaks'—drop-outs from one way of running things—drop-ins to another (and a better, we think, otherwise we would not be doing it).

When Sally and I started living this sort of life twenty-three years ago at the Broom we were rare birds indeed—I should think just about unique. We were amusing oddities and everybody was rather fond of us, in a patronizing sort of way. 'Of course it's ridiculous to grow your own food,' people would say, 'when you can get it so easily from the shop.' But, nevertheless, people would come and look at us, and think what fun it must be even if it was silly, and I would give talks about it all on the radio, and people would write to me and say they'd often thought about living like that too, but of course it wasn't possible.

Then, as I mentioned in Chapter 1, way back in about 1960 I found that there were a lot of people living like us in the United States, and that they even published a paper: the *Green Revolution* (nothing to do with that *other* upstart, 'green revolution' which consists of breeding wheat and rice that would grow large yields if fed with even larger quantities of scarce nitrogenous fertilizer). When I heard of these people I felt like a man with two heads must feel, who thinks he is the only such man in the world and then hears that there are other people with two heads as well, on the other side of the world. It was quite exciting.

But now we are quite commonplace. Of course people say to me: 'It's all right for *you* to live like this because you have a good income from your books.' 'Well aren't I lucky?' I always reply. But the other freaks around us—they don't write books (although I have a suspicion some of them would like to). And they all have to earn 'bread' somehow—the sort of thing hippies call 'bread'—i.e. money. You can be as self-sufficient as you like, you can grow every ounce of your own food, weave your clothes from the wool off your own sheep, drink dandelion coffee and have no mortgage but you *still*, in this world of ours, have to have some money. Not much, but some.

Well, here is a short list of what a few of my fellow drop-ins do to earn money. Wood-turning. Potting. Wood-carving. Carpentry. Boat-building. Wheel-wrighting. Designing and selling post cards. Bee-keeping. Growing soft fruit and selling it on a pick-it-yourself basis. Making spinning wheels. Restoring antiques. Publishing a line of short guides to Pembrokeshire. Publishing books on Persian carpets. Working for neighbouring big farmers. Running a boarding kennels. Teaching horse riding. Practising as a lawyer. As an architect. As a dentist. Growing vegetables and selling them out of the back of an old van at cattle markets. Doing leather work. Making jewellery. Weaving.

But gradually I get the feeling that this growing army is invading every corner of trade and production. I even met a young man yesterday who wants to get a schooner and *trade*. He wants to sail to countries like the Mediterranean ones where they grow things we can't (wine, olives, rice) loaded with stuff we can produce but they can't, sell his cargo there, buy a cargo with the money, and sail back. Sounds ridiculous—but consider, if it is possible, how many agents, brokers, insurers, dock authorities, dockers, handlers, lorry drivers, port officials, etc. etc. etc. it would cut out. It struck me that this is going *forward* to real trade: simple, direct, purposeful and useful. We don't want too much trade in this world, we are better without it. It is ridiculous for a whole generation of freaks in Britain to grow up thinking that the only good food to eat is 'brown rice', for example. We don't grow rice in Britain. We grow wheat, and should eat that—it's a much better food than rice anyway. Then it's ridiculous to see one ship loaded with new cars steaming from Calais to Dover and another loaded with new cars steaming the other way. But *some* trade is desirable, and enriches life. For example, I like grape wine and I like olive oil and I am willing to exchange, say, salt fish for it, or bacon or ham, or butter, commodities much in demand in Portugal and terribly expensive there. Well, what's wrong with that? That's reasonable trade, and if some young man comes along with a schooner, and is willing to do the carrying for me, he is doing both me and the Portuguese a signal service.

But we freaks, as I say, are gradually invading every sphere of industry and trade. You may ask—what is the difference between a man who publishes guide books and calls himself a 'self-supporter' and one who does the same thing and calls himself an industrialist? Well, there is a big difference, for the first does not have to earn so much money, and he spends much of each day doing healthy and pleasant work in the fresh air instead of hunched over a desk. He can afford to please himself as to what he publishes, for he doesn't have that overriding need to find several pounds every day to feed his wife and his family. Also he can play it how he likes—spend as much time at this trade and as much time on his holding as the whim dictates. It is also a matter of state of mind. The self-supporter is consciously withdrawing from industrial, high technological society because he thinks it is ugly, boring, polluting and dangerous. He cannot see how the herding of mankind into cities of ten million people, and getting food and water to them there, and carrying away their wastes, can possibly be sustained for much longer. We 'freaks' believe quite seriously that we are building an alternative society, an alternative agriculture and industry and commerce, an alternative life style; we are mad on making land produce much food with a small input of power and chemicals (it is the small input that seems so important to us); we are keen to build small-scale, humane, rural industries, where the workers all have a share and can feel proud of what they are producing; we are keen to *reduce* our needs to the simple and essential. We don't think that the good life has to be sustained by complicated and expensive artifacts. I can go into a shop in a city—practically any shop except butcher, baker, fishmonger and greengrocer—and eliminate, in my mind at least, nine-tenths of the goods in it as being worthless, redundant and a waste of human time. We believe that materialism is a disease, like cancer, or tuberculosis. We are searching for a cure.

We still make all sorts of mistakes, we take wrong turnings, people get their little bits of land and do not know how to farm them, some are laughed at by their square neighbours, some resort to such sad measures as going on the dole or national assistance, some take to drugs, some go mad, some go home to the job in Daddy's office. But our army, tiny now, gets bigger, stronger, more self-confident, learns how to do more things, and people like Sally and me, instead of being utterly alone in an alien world, now feel no longer alone. And it's better to be a member of a small army which is getting bigger, than of a big army that is getting smaller. We freaks have no doubt whatever in our minds to whom the future belongs, if future there is going to be.

Well, the only way I could make money was by writing, and also broadcasting and television work.

I wasn't bad at sound radio, having done it for years, but at first I was very bad at television. I'm not sure that I very much like people who are good at television. The professional 'personality', like the successful 'disc jockey', tends to be a very unpleasant individual. For a person to find himself famous for being something very difficult, like a musician, a surgeon, an engineer, a painter, is good for him, and most such people seem modest and have integrity. But for somebody suddenly to find himself famous for *nothing at all*—just because he has an engaging way with him before a microphone or in front of a camera and not because he has mastered any particular skill, is very bad for him and sad indeed. The quality of our 'personalities' is a measure of the inanity of our society. The young people who gain enormous, if transitory, world-wide fame by pop music, when they have absolutely no musical knowledge or training at all, by dressing up in funny clothes and screaming into a microphone about their relations with their 'babies', at the same time knocking hell out of the steel strings of an electric guitar, are in exactly the same class. Fame does you good—if it is fame for being good at some skill or discipline you have really become a master at. Fame that happens for nothing, by luck as it were, is about the worst thing that can happen to a man or woman.

The last thing I wanted, or will ever want, is fame, and I find

it acutely embarrassing when some stranger comes up to me
and says: 'I saw you on the telly last night.' But I needed money,
the telly was a way of getting it, and I used to go away from
home, often for weeks at a time, to make sound programmes or
films, or do research for the guide books that I was writing.

I made one series of sound programmes by getting myself to
Llangollen, in North Wales, and following on foot the route
taken a hundred odd years before by George Borrow, after
which he wrote that incomparable travel book: *Wild Wales*.
Borrow is a master of topographical description, and it was
possible, with his book in my knapsack, to follow his route to a
yard, identify every house and building, tree (if it was still
there) and rock that he described. I knocked on every door he
knocked on (in a very few cases there was no door left to knock
on—the house was ruined or gone) and was amazed to find how
little rural and mountain Wales has changed in over a hundred
years. Every night I slept in the same pub or inn that Borrow
had slept in—often, according to the landlord, in the same bed.
After a few days of this I got an extraordinary feeling of having
dropped back into the past. The people I met, in any place
that Borrow had described, knew about him and often talked
about him as though he had passed by the day before. I met a
man who kept the California Inn in Anglesey. Borrow had
described how he had met a sea captain, retired from having
made money on the California run, constructing this very
building. For some reason, when Borrow had addressed the
man in Welsh he had replied in Spanish.

'Borrow was a damned liar!' said the landlord of the pub
when I told him about this. 'He addressed my grandfather in
Spanish—just to show how clever he was! And he got the surprise of his life when my grandfather answered him in Spanish
better than his own, for he had learnt it in the California trade.'
Whatever the wrongs and rights of this story, it did give me
once again, the impression that I had crashed the time-barrier.
The landlord then got a neighbour from over the road—another
descendant of the old sailor who had built the pub—and the
latter showed me a fine model of the ship the sea captain had
made his money in, and a family Bible. The story of the latter
was that the captain had presented it to the local Chapel. In

his retirement he had taken to trading with a small ketch and had been caught, and fined, for smuggling salt. Because of this heinous offence (or because, at any rate, he had been caught) he was expelled from the Chapel. 'Right,' said the old sea captain, when he heard this sentence; he stumped up the aisle, took his Bible from the lectern, and stumped off with it, and there it still is with his descendant.

The sound programmes were a success. I carried a tape recorder with me (which got heavier and heavier the further I carried it for I really *did* walk) and recorded people all along the route. And then the BBC asked me to do a series of television programmes on the same route.

This was great fun. The producer was a splendid man named Selwyn Roderick, with whom I had made a film or two before, and the camera crews, although they changed for every programme, were for the most part made up of fine lusty fellows, good at sinking a pint of beer or chasing a wench (some of them of course were *very* steady fellows), but all good company and fun to be with. We stayed in pubs—often the pub that George Borrow stayed in when he passed that way and, because we were filming and bringing a bit of excitement to the area, the local people came around, and were very friendly in their welcome, and very often it was difficult to get to bed. There was one pub up in North Wales that we got to like so much that we lingered on there for much longer than we should have done so that we were having to drive miles every day to get to the filming. There was one huge room for bawling Welsh hymns and another smaller room where the finest *penillion* singing was performed, and a lady, one of the waitresses in the dining-room, played a superb Welsh harp. This pub, like many a country pub still, thank God, knew nothing of the licensing laws, and singing and talking often went on far into the night. I will never forget the landlord—a splendid high priest of a landlord—one of the great landlords of all time—saying to our one sober member, who had complained the night before at the late hours kept by the other guests in the bar right under his bedroom: 'What's the trouble about? I had 'em all out of the bar by three o'clock!'

Filming is really a tedious job, for to get the simplest sequence

'in the can' every one of a very large number of factors has to
be just right; thus often some simple action has to be repeated
a dozen times. The first 'take' is cut because the sound engineer
says he's not happy about wind in the mike. The second because a car goes by along a road in the background—the first
car, apparently, for a hundred years. The third because an
aeroplane goes over. The fourth because the sun goes in—or
comes out—in the middle of it and upsets the lighting. The
fifth because the man in front of the camera (in other words
me) forgets his lines, fluffs, or says the wrong thing. Film costs
money, and film crews cost a lot of time, and all these delays
are infuriating, and it is very hard to keep up one's spontaneity
time after time with the producer shouting 'Cut!' in the middle
of one's finest sentence perfectly delivered.

I remember one ludicrous scene when I had to appear over
a cairn of rock on a mountain, in a howling gale of wind (one
could hardly stand up against it and the camera had to be wedged
against a rock), waving my umbrella (George Borrow carried
an umbrella so I did too), and declaim a ludicrous verse that
Borrow declaimed a hundred and twenty years before:

> 'Who lies 'neath the carn on the headland hoar
> 'His hand still clutching his broad claymore,
> 'Is it Beli, the son of Gelli Mawr?'

I repeated this piece of typically Borrovian nonsense a dozen
times, having to climb back down the cairn and up again almost hurled backwards by the wind and somehow contrive to
keep my balance in the stupendous gale (the Air Ministry spoke
of gusts of a hundred miles an hour that day), waving my umbrella in the teeth of it, and shouting the verse again. We had to
cut for camera shake, for excessive wind in the mike (that over
and over again of course), for me slipping, for me looking even
more ridiculous than the occasion called for, for the cameraman
not being ready, for the film running out, but finally we got it
all right—everything perfect—a marvel I thought if there ever
was one. But, without my conscious mind having anything to
do with it, some devil within me seized the controls, and I
bellowed:

Who lies 'neath the bed of the aging Whore
His hand yet clutching his broad claymore
Is it Selwyn, the son of Roderick Mawr?

Nobody thought it was funny, excepting of course myself.
And the next three takes were spoiled by aeroplanes.

I cannot pretend that making such films was not fun though,
despite the tedium. But I cannot pretend that I really wanted to
do it either. My heart was back at the farm. I wanted to go on
fencing, and draining, and clearing, and building up our flocks
and herds, and getting more land under the plough, growing
more crops. Further, I wanted to be with Sally and my children.
But alas, as time went on it was more that I wanted to be with
my children. Sally seemed estranged from me. We are now no
longer married, and are almost as close as two people can be
(without even thinking of going to bed with each other) but
at that time we were drifting rapidly apart. Sally has told me
since that she found it hurtful that I went away so often and for
so long, and she had to steel herself to endure my absences,
and she could only do this by ceasing to be dependent on me,
and thus to love me. For my part the time came when, on my
wanderings, I no longer looked forward to going home. And
Sally had to take over more and more of the working of the farm
—perforce. And then I would come back and she would resent
it, perhaps, if I took over the controls again, and I was forced
either to go against her wishes or else just to leave all the farming
to her and merely be a labourer and do what I was told. Life
was becoming very unhappy.

So I began to live more and more for my roamings, knocking
about the countryside in a picaresque sort of way and making
all sorts of friends in all sorts of places, and if I did not feel
wanted at home at least I did in a score of places in England and
Wales, where I had friends, of all kinds and conditions, who were
pleased to see me and welcomed me in.

A Night at the Diglis Hotel

Oh Holy Mother Corporation!
The sacred BBC!
Had smiled upon the least of her children

None more, none less, none other than me
Oh would I make a recorded programme
About some horrible motorway
About to blast over hills and valley
Well yes I would. I needed the pay.
I'd start at Worcester in Worcestershire
That ancient, honorable, venerable town
At least it was when I went there that time
Before its inhabitants knocked it down.
And I was to walk the route of the freeway
Carrying a tape machine under my arm
And talk to the people about to be ousted
From house and cottage and manse and farm.
They had booked me in at the Diglis Hotel—just think of it!
There's posh. I got out of the train at the station and spurned
To take taxi (the cost of it) walked through the streets of the
    centre
Till I came to the ancient heart of the city—the heart now
No longer. And passing an old pub—a pub since gone under
    the bulldozer
The Farrier's Arms if it serves me, my memory—heard music
Mouth music, if you know what that means. Were Gypsies—
    Tziganos.
So quick in I went. 'Come in brother! Make room at the fire
    for the *Mush*
There!' And so glass in hand I heard music, saw dancing,
    heard songs both
In English and Romany, heard the plaintive mouth-organ,
    was happy.
The man I sat next to was Charlie, an old *Didikai* man
A tatter. A ragman. A good'un. A rough 'un. A wrong 'un. A
Bad 'un. A drunk 'un but by God he could drink and could
    take it
And give it, and he drank, and I drank, we all drank till the
    place was aroar.
'Now can I have your glasses please!' cried the landlord. 'Tis
    time please!
'Tis midnight! Drink up now! We've had a good evening—
    they'll book me!'

'Can you tell me the way', I said nicely, to Charlie, 'to the
    Diglis Hotel?'
'The Diglis? A job, mate? You want to be careful. The *gavs*
    here are hot mush!'
'Oh dear no! I'm straight, mate! To sleep, mate. Booked in,
    man. A room man.'
'To *sleep*? In the Diglis? You means to pay luvva! Oh *dordi*! I
Knowed you was flash man but Lawdi you don't want to go
    there man
Now me and me missus we's poor, man but we's have got a
    home, man
And we's have got a bed, man—you're right welcome to
    sleep *mush*.'
So some cider we bought for his missus, in bottles, and into
    the midnight we
Sortied. It drizzled. And down to the river he led me, old
    Severn
Old Hafren. The water looked murky and oily, the midnight
    was dark and was lonely
We crossed it, old Hafren, and came to a land of hereafter, a
    land of
For ever, a land now of never, a lost land, a was land
Where the mighty bulldozer was resting from smashing and
    crashing
The houses were empty, deserted, the windows all boarded
Or smashed, and our footsteps re-echoed 'tween Factory Act
    housing now gutted
And hopeless. At the end of a row was a house barricaded
    and boarded.
'We's here John. Come quietly. We's ain't rightly 'sposed to
    be here though
The *gavs* mustn't see us.' We crept round the back of the
    house then
Tapped lightly. Heard drawing of bolts and much wrenching
    and old hag
Peered out to the darkness. Went in and with bolting and
    banging
The door was nailed into its framing. A problem arose in my
    mind then

E   111

Now what when I wanted to pee? (This would happen in due
course of nature.)
The back room was piled high with ragging and tagging it
reached to
The ceiling. A huge double bed filled the front room with
space for
An armchair and a fire that burned brightly consuming the
house for
Old lady went up to the top floor with hatchet and smashing
And splintering told plainly her work there the floor she was
wrenching
Our fire to replenish. Her cider we opened and drank it
To help her and Charlie told stories, and newspaper cuttings
He showed me. 'I just ain't no scholard', he told me, 'Please
read them!'
I read 'em and wondered—they were all about Charlie, his
misdeeds
His violence—how policemen had caught him how beaks had
annoyed him
His list of convictions as long as your arm.
'That's right, man! You got it! He reads it out splendid!
And he said
And I said and they said and we said and that's right I hit
him and
Bloomin' nigh killed him and when I got out man I did it again!'
And Seymour began to feel—well—put it mildly—well not to
be wildly
Concerned for his safety—but wallet I'd flashed it and bank
had just
Stashed it and what if I lost it and what would it cost if I
Came to some harm? But 'Drink some more cider!' and 'Sing
wes a song John!'
And 'Has ye heard this one!' and the night wore along. Then
nature asserted
Its rigid compulsions and plenary expulsions for I
Wanted to pee.
But so, thank God, did my host.
So unboltings and bangings, and hammering nails outings and
wrenchings and

Clenchings and we opened the door. And out in the drizzle
  we both did a
Pizzle and the old lady shameless did that which was nameless
And then we went into the house just once more. And make
  fast the door boys and
Think of the law boys they'll ne'er let us poor boys sleep
  peaceful the night.
Now after we'd finished the cider
My host put his glass down and said:
'The old woman can sleep on the rags John
While me and you'll sleep on the bed.'
Oh he wasn't a queer Sir—just kind to his peer Sir but I'm
Always the gent Sir and will be to my grave. So his bed I
Declined Sir being far too refined Sir and the rags I ab-
Horred Sir so I chose the armchair. Now the rags they
  weren't harmful
So they gathered an armful and covered me up with 'em right
  up to my hair.

They got into bed and blew out the candle. The fire flickered
—the house continued slowly to consume itself. Sleep eluded
me. Outside I remembered the Severn flowed stealthily onward
to the sea. Silence except for the snoring of my companions.
Then they woke up. They whispered together but though not a
yard away from my head I could not hear their confabulation. I
heard rustling—Charlie was stealthily getting out of bed. I
remembered those reports of mayhem—my wallet—nay, the
BBC's tape machine. Cautiously I pushed the heap of rags away
from me and prepared to assume a posture of defence.

The bed sprung as Charlie swung his feet upon the ground
The rags fell in a senseless heap as Seymour with a bound
Leapt to his feet for life was sweet—he intended to sell it dear
'Oh light the bloody candle, Mag!' cried Charlie loud and clear.
'It's all right, mate—I know it's late
But I've got to pee again
And one thing is clear—I'll do it here
And not in the bleeding rain!'

After both had relieved themselves, in the plastic washing-up
bowl, and the old lady had grumbled at the fuss and disturbance,

they went to their places of repose again, Seymour much com-
forted. Oh what silly imaginings and false alarms! But suddenly,
outside in the ruined and debris-strewn street—came heavy foot
tramps. At last I thought I understood it all.

For there's going to be a shoot-in
Or at least they'll put the boot-in
Old Charlie's in cahoots
With men in heavy boots
I'll be floating down the Severn
On my bloody way to Heaven . . .
But last time Charlie had nailed up the door
I'd seen the hammer put down on the floor
If I could find it I'd use it well
And send one or two of the buggers to hell!
But just as I was thinking I'm about to lose my fleece
Old Maggie gave a whisper: 'Sssh, Charlie—it's the police!'
And the *gavs* it was, and they hammered and rattled and
    banged at the door
And then went away, and came back no more.
And that's really the end of the story of my night at the
    Diglis Hotel.
I slept for the rest of the night and I slept—very well.
And now I come to the moral and point of this lengthy
    narration
Oh the infinite strangeness of the human nation!
After some tea in the morning, with condensed milk, white
    bread and marge
I picked up my tape recorder and prepared to go at large.
'Maggie,' I said 'Would you care to let me buy you a drink?
Here's a quid.' 'Now, John,' said Charlie, 'What do you think
Wes are? Beggars? Well maybe wes ain't millionaires
But what little we has got you did ought to know that we
    shares
With our pals. Now Maggie—you cut our old brother here a
    good hunk of bread and cheese
To take on his journey.'
And of all this
You can make what you please.

I had always counted a number of Gypsy people among my friends, and, as I roamed about England and Wales, making programmes for the BBC, or collecting material for guide books, etc. I found I spent more and more time in the company of Gypsies. I just seemed to have a natural affinity with them, that was all. I got to know one family of them, the Boswells—Gordon Sylvester Boswell and Mabel his wife, and their children and relations—so well that I still look on Gordon—or Uncle Gordon as I think of him in my mind, for he is older than I am, and Gypsies give old people they respect the title of Uncle or Aunt— as the staunchest of my friends, and nowhere do I feel happier than at their great scrapyard outside Spalding, in Lincolnshire. I helped Uncle Gordon, by recording his words on a tape recorder for three weeks and then having them typed out, to produce the greatest and best book ever to appear about the Gypsy people: *The Book of Boswell: The Life of a Gypsy Man.*

The BBC asked me to do a fairly profound study of Gypsies for a series of sound programmes in the old Third Programme, and for this I had to read everything in English about Gypsies, and meet the members of that extraordinary body The Gypsy Lore Society, alas now defunct, as well as a great many of the more interesting or influential Gypsies in the country. I helped my friend Phillip Donnellan, a film producer of the BBC in Birmingham, make *Where do we go from here?* which I consider to be the best film ever to be made about Gypsies (and about the only one of any seriousness about British Gypsies).

The prejudice against Gypsies, or all Travelling People, in these islands is pathological. It is xenophobia at its most extreme and sordid.

The common complaint of the ignorant is: 'There are no true Gypsies left nowadays.' What they mean is that Gypsies no longer go about in horse-drawn wagons and dress in picturesque clothing. There are not only plenty of true Gypsies around today but probably more than there ever were. Many of them live in trailer-caravans, or living vans (they hate the word 'caravan' as applied to a living trailer and only use it when speaking to non-Gypsies), many live in houses—some very posh ones. The fact that people other than Gypsies also live in living-trailers doesn't make the true Gypsies any less Gypsies. The word 'Traveller' has been coined in recent years to cover all travelling people, Gypsies included. True Gypsies have an ambivalent attitude to the word *Gypsy*. They use it among themselves with a great, if rather defiant, pride. They have immense pride in their race, considering themselves far superior to *Gaujos*, which is what they call non-Gypsies. But they don't like being called Gypsies by non-Gypsies, because the word has acquired a pejorative meaning.

The Gypsies are a distinct ethnic group and their history is known with some precision: there is no mystery about their origins at all, at least until we get back to the thirteenth century. They are descended from a race, or tribe, of people who roamed about India, getting their livings by making music, horse-dealing, blacksmithing and kindred trades. Their direct descendants can be seen to this day and to anyone who knows European Gypsies are immediately recognizable for what they are. Riding through the Punjab once I came upon a large band of them, encamped outside a big Jat village, with a train of perhaps two dozen ox carts to carry their belongings. The men were smiths, and were working busily at primitive forges doing all the blacksmith work for the village probably for the next year. Having done it they would move on to the next village, and do their blacksmithing work for them. The sort of jobs they do are the rather specialist ones that occur too infrequently to give a settled tradesman a living. In these days of universal mobility you can jump in to a car or on to a bus and drive twenty miles to have a kettle mended (in any case you would throw it away and buy another one in Woolworths) but this was not always so. You would keep it until the gypsies came along.

In Ceylon I have frequently seen bands of people—so obviously Gypsies that they would not have looked out of place at Appleby

Fair—travelling the country with portable huts made of *cadjan*, or woven coconut fronds, loaded on donkeys. These people have many resources (telling fortunes and necromancy of one sort or another—in other words exploiting the feeling of mystery that surrounds travelling people—are generally among them) but their chief stock-in-trade is snake-charming. They will knock on the door of a credulous householder and tell him his garden is full of poisonous snakes. 'Rubbish!' says the householder. And the Gypsies take him out, and go round his garden, and 'charm' half a dozen cobras and other venemous reptiles out of various holes and crannies and put them away in baskets. The householder, so incredibly simple that he doesn't know what is happening to him, gladly pays them some money, and then pays them some more when they give a performance of making the snakes 'dance' to the music of their rude flutes. The reason the snakes were there, of course, is that the Gypsies put them there; the reason that they didn't bite the Gypsies is that they had had their poison sacs removed; the reason that they 'dance' to the music is that the charmer has a coloured rag held in his knee, and he waves this rhythmically in front of the snake's nose and the snake, half hypnotized, waves in answer.

I remember, as a little *Gaujo* child living in the Manor House of an Essex village, walking along a lane with my nanny and suddenly seeing an encampment of Gypsies. They looked so impossibly romantic that they gave me a strange feeling of yearning (to go off with them), amazement (that there should be such beings in our civilized, settled, world), and wonder. I had the feeling that I could never, ever, make contact with them, for they would not accept me for one instant. But they *were* romantic, with their fine multi-coloured horses, their painted wagons, long lean lurcher dogs chained up under them, fine-looking dark women in brightly coloured long dresses with scarves round their heads, indolent lounging men with horsey-looking clothes, broad-brimmed hats, and handkerchiefs round their necks. While they were there there would be a feeling of excitement in the village: 'the Gypsies are here!' people would say, and one would sense this feeling of slightly alarmed excitement. I believe that one could classify the human race into two groups by their attitude towards Gypsies. There is the attitude that I should call the 'town councillor attitude' of: 'these people are different from us, therefore they must be driven away, or made to conform', and the opposite attitude of many a countryman—and townsman too—of 'these people are alive and different, and therefore interesting, so let us be tolerant to them, and not mind if they pinch a chicken or two'. Not that I am alleging that any Travelling man ever *did* steal a chicken, or anything else for that matter. Of course, if a pheasant actually flew into a Gypsy's hand . . . An old Gypsy man told me that when he was driving along a country lane, and chanced to observe a pheasant's nest over the hedge, he would send his wife in there to relieve herself. She would squat down over the nest, her long skirt about her, and what if a gamekeeper did come along, or was in hiding—she was relieving her nature, wasn't she, and the man being a gentleman would keep away. Later the Gypsy man would sell the pheasant eggs back to the gamekeeper.

Now the Gypsies, or a branch of them, left India in the thirteenth century, moving over into Persia. This is known quite definitely from Persian writings of the time. 'A nation of travelling musicians and dancers has entered our dominions from Hind,' wrote the scribe of the Iranian king. They were welcome at first, then became a nuisance (one gathers there were a lot of them), and spread on further westwards. Their progress through the Near East and Europe can be followed accurately by contemporary accounts. They travelled in large bands—hundreds strong—and gained admittance to many countries by calling themselves 'The Kings of Lower Egypt', and telling some cock and bull story about how their ancestors had forged the nails of the Cross, and for this sin (although an unwitting one) they had been condemned by God to roam for seven hundred years. They had letters (forged of course) from the Pope, ordering all authorities in the lands through which they wished to wander to give them hospitality and free passage. European records of the fourteenth, fifteenth and sixteenth centuries are full of references to these 'Egyptians' as they were called—mostly describing their depredations and how they were being moved on. Wherever they went they suffered severe persecution, but they were—and are—masters at slipping away unnoticed. They don't oppose or defy authority, so much as use their ready tongues to disarm it, or their mobility and secretiveness to slide out from under it. Which is why they resent so much the current tendency of Irish Tinkers (a distinct race altogether, with no connection with true Gypsies at all) to band together and defy the police or the authorities who want to move them. The Gypsies have not survived outside India for seven hundred years by using violence. They have their own distinctive language, and there are still one or two Gypsies in Britain (I know one of them—a knife-grinder in Liverpool) who can talk the complete, grammatically correct, highly inflected language—with not an English word among it. Most British Gypsies, however, know comparatively few words of their old language, and simply interlard their own particular, very racy and old-fashioned English with enough Romany words to make themselves un-intelligible to *Gaujos*. They are very secretive about their language and most of them deny all knowledge of it, even though they have quite a lot. On the Continent Romany is far more intact, although there are many branches of it. Different tribes of Gypsies on the Continent (and they really do go in tribes there) speak different dialects of Romany, and the route of each tribe, on its way from India to its present place of abode, can be followed exactly by philologists according to how many words of the nations through which the tribe passed have been taken into the dialect: but the basis of Romany is Hindi, and if you know the latter you will have little difficulty with the former.

In the radio programmes I made about Gypsy people, I tried to draw attention to the fact that they are a distinct race, have as much right to their way of life as we have to ours, and should be respected. They are, to my mind, an embellishment to a country—they are a fun people. Further, the work they do in Britain today is very useful. A high proportion of them are scrap-dealers, and what could be a more useful activity than that? There is much talk by 'environmentalists' these days of the need for 'recycling'. Well, Gypsy scrap-dealers and totters (rag collectors) have been doing nothing else for years. Our country-side would be covered with old junk if Gypsy scrappers didn't come along and clear it up, often paying good prices for it, and take it off to the steel mills to be recycled. Junkyards look untidy, of course, and *Gaujos* say: 'look at the filthy Gypsies', but they forget that without them the whole country would be a junk yard. And when people say to me that Gypsies make a mess I answer: 'Yes, but look at the mess *we* make!' At least Gypsies don't pollute the air and drench the land and waters with poisons, throw up huge hideous factories and office buildings, rape the good land with motorways. Their mess is very minor and transitory compared with ours.

Anyway, I flogged about the country with a tape recorder, and put the Romany point of view as well as I could. When you meet Gypsies a lot you come to know them immediately—no matter how well they are disguised. You get on the same wave-length somehow. And, without trying to, you take on the aura of that nation—so much so that you arouse immediate interest when you walk into a Gypsy circle—they see you are not a Gypsy and yet they see you are not just an ordinary *Gaujo* either.

'Hullo, Brother—what are you into?'

'Oh—just dodging about.'

'Scrap?'

'Oh no—just trying to get a bob or two.'

'Times is hard—eh?'

The other day I happened to be driving in my old van up in the Midlands of England (I do still sometimes cross Offa's Dyke) and I found myself near the horrible 'new town' of Dawley. I went into a pub I knew and enquired after a friend of mine.

'Nelson?' said the landlord. 'He was in here the other night. Quite a tribe of 'em.' And he told me where he was.

I drove away, turned off the road on to a rough track which wound through slag heaps and old mine-dumps, past some rows of derelict miners' cottages; some tall brick chimneys rose up high and gaunt from the scrub that was struggling to establish itself over the ravaged soil—it was a landscape of sterility and desolation. The industrial revolution had started here—had passed on and left this wilderness, almost beautiful in its stark-ness and decay.

I rounded a slag heap and beheld a great heap of scrapped

motor cars—gutted and burnt out and flung one on top of the other. The heap was swarming with children—they were clambering all over it.

Because they were Gypsy children they saw me as soon as I saw them—and saw who I was—and came rushing and shouting towards me. Their reactions were split-second—they had never been dulled and deadened by years of peering at books.

They besieged my van. They were as filthy as any children could ever be—but *black*. 'John—John—it's John!' they shouted.

I let 'em all in and they filled the van. They were in frenzied excitement—not because of my arrival but because they are always excited. 'That's Nels's van John—that 'n there—he's there! Nels is there! His brother too—Perce—I'm his kid. You remembers me, mister? I'm Perce's kid—that's me sister!' But they are all shouting at once.

Nelson and his wife are by their trailer caravan—not a 'flash' trailer—they are not rich people. There is a fire on the ground outside on which Caroline is heating water to wash clothes. Indeed, clothes need washing. They are delighted to see me.

'Do they bother you much?' I ask them. This is a ritual question, and 'they' means the police—or the 'sanitary inspectors' —those men who—where you or I would see the stars and the unconquerable spirit of man—can only see ordure.

'We got to shift,' says Nelson. 'Given us 'til Friday.'

What bloody harm are they doing here? I think.

We have a ritual cup of tea. We drink it out of just the ordinary Crown Derby—a cup and saucer worth ten pounds! Nelson and Caroline may be poor, but they have the ordinary amenities of life. If one of these cups was washed in the clothes-washing bowl by mistake it would have to be smashed: it would be for ever unclean. Such is the Gypsy tradition.

There are other trailers nearby—perhaps a dozen within view. A crowd collects. I know some of them—know of more.

We sit on old boxes near a fire and eat hunks of white bread with fried bacon on them. We talk of friends and of enemies. We talk of horses and of dogs. We go over to another trailer to see a lurcher. Fine-looking brindle bitch—favouring the greyhound a bit too much.

'Give you five bar for it!' I say to the owner.

'What, gen'leman? I wouldn't sell that bitch for a thousand pounds'—he was seething with just indignation—'I wouldn't take nothing for her—didn't she kill four hares in half an hour, Alg? I tell you what—nothing'd make me sell that dog—I've won hundreds wi' 'er. Ha'nt I Alg? Alg'll bear me out.'

'Come on, John—offer 'im a tenner—he'll have a deal. Have a deal with the *mush*!'

'I wouldn't take a hundred pound for 'er. Alg—fetch that hare what she killed yesterday—show the man.'

We admire the hare, admire the bitch, the owner decides he wouldn't take fifty for her, but would plainly take ten if it were offered, which it isn't, and we wander off to play pitch and toss with some kids. The men and the boys play together completely as equals—shouting at one another uninhibitedly and occasionally accusing each other loudly of cheating. We try a ·22 rifle—smashing bottles with it which are flung up into the air. We throw knives into crown beer bottle tops stuck into a post. We try our skill with a catapult. At all these activities I am hopelessly outclassed by anybody over five years old.

Some men are working—some are playing—some are lounging by the fire. Perce drives off with a high load of scrap metal in his Bedford truck.

Suddenly we hear a motor coming. Everybody keeps quiet—looks alert. Strangers. Danger perhaps.

A big truck roars round the corner—heads straight towards us. 'It's Tisale! It's Tisale! Missus and chavis!' someone cries.

'Good God, I ain't sin him for months—he's got a new wagon!' says Nelson.

The new truck is 'flash'—varnished teak sides, plenty of chrome about, tasselled crimson curtains in the cab windows, chrome-plated figures of horses pulling trotting buggies stuck to the bonnet.

It comes racing up—pulls to a stop with a groan of brakes, and a handsome black-haired man leaps out—followed by a pretty woman and four children. The man walks towards us with a cowboy swagger—the woman and kids following more sedately behind.

'How you gettin' on?' says Nelson.

'Knockin' along. Just make a living. Nothin' about. Bin to you yet?'

'Got to move Friday. Council men. Where you *atched*?'

'Know where Uncle Charlie used to stop? Just this side Stourport? Bin there a week.'

'Bin to you?'

'*Muskro* come. Give us a day though. Bin there a week since. Thinkin' of moving up Manchester way.'

'No good there. Too many fuckin' Irish.'

Everybody is watching. There is an air of encounter. What's going to happen next? Who will come? Where shall we be to-morrow? Where do we go from here?

The pubs are open.

'John—you go with me Uncle Nels—I'll drive your van!'

'Come in—plenty of room—we can get a few more in!'

We drove off in a convoy—every vehicle overloaded—me squashed in with Nelson and his lot—some wild young boy with no licence driving my van. Little kids run whooping alongside getting in the way. 'Go home you little bastards!' shouts Nels. 'Ain't yous got more sense? Yous got no more sense than fuckin' animals!' 'Bring us back some fuckin' beer!' the dear little mites shout in reply.

We stamp into the pub and shout for beer. Everybody clamours to pay—we must all show how rich we are. Heavy rolls of notes are flashed. This is one of the few pubs around here which admits Travellers. The men clamour at the bar—the women sit in a row against the wall, behind a table, waiting for their drinks. Every now and then one of them discreetly shoves a pound note into the hand of her man: not all of us have got note rolls to flash.

'Good God, gen'lman—you ain't drinkin' nothin'!' says a stranger to me.

'He ain't no gen'lman!' says Perce. 'He's a *kushti mush* same as what we are.'

'Gi's a song Perce!' shouts someone. 'Come on—gi' 'im order —gi's a song!'

And Percy gives us a song, and several more, and he knows scores of songs, including several old countrymen *used* to sing—

for the Gypsies, being illiterate, can remember things and are the archives of the people. Settled men forget their heritage. The Nomad remembers. He remembers—and remembers right through—every song of note and value from the days of Tudor England (when Gypsies were first reported here) to the latest 'number' (not song) of the Americanized yearn-merchants.

A girl sings the latest 'pop number' that she has heard from a juke box. Unlike the *Gaujo*, or non-Gypsy, teenager she *knows* it—right through. She mimics the bogus American accent of the original singer perfectly—and yet she sings in a voice so harsh and eastern and lovely that you think of some Spanish *flamenco* singer. She transforms rubbish into beauty.

A man pulls out an old half-broken mouth organ—plays a step tune—another gets an old tin beer tray from the counter and begins to beat it like a drum—a third borrows two spoons from the landlord and rattles them together and soon there is a rhythm that takes you straight back to the plains of India. A man gets up and step dances—a woman leaps in front of him and follows him step for step.

We all get pretty rowdy. I am accused of having designs on Nelson's wife. Raucous remarks are made—these people have no inhibitions about the *bawdy*. There is tapping on the window —small dirty faces peer in. Perce buys a flagon of cider and some packets of crisps and shoves them out to waiting children.

'Time' comes—we are chucked out. We go to the vans and lorries lugging cases of beer. Back we go—at a reckless speed— to the camp among the slag heaps. When we arrive our drivers slam on the brakes like cowboys pulling their broncos up in a film and out we get and a big fire is lit.

We crowd round it—some sitting on old tins or boxes—some on the ground—some standing up. The children—all of them right down to babes in arms—are with us. There are more children than adults. They join in absolutely freely and un-inhibitedly in everything the adults do. Boys are busy opening beer bottles—some of them with their teeth. Miraculously the bottles seem to disappear from the cases.

'Stop them little *chavis*!' shouts someone. 'They'll drink the fuckin' lot!'

But stop them we cannot. Little kids of three and four are

running about drinking from the bottle—running away from older brothers and sisters who are trying to snatch the bottles from them. But all is good humour—laughter. Older kids see that the younger ones get a fair share.

We all do in fact.

'Gi's a dance Liza—Liza, gi's a step!' calls someone. An old piece of board is pulled from under a caravan—a piece of board carried about expressly for this purpose. It is thrown on the ground higgledy-piggledy, and Liza—an old lady looking like a story-book Gypsy—says: 'Who'll tune for me—who'll tune for me! Lija—you tune for me!'

Lija makes 'mouth-music', very skilfully, and old Liza dances —rattling her feet on the board with terrible speed in spite of her seventy-five years.

Dancing over, there is a bedlam of shouting and swearing and people trying to get other people to sing and laughter and shouting at the *chavis* and the children shouting back—and suddenly one becomes aware of something remote—far-out— far-away—beautiful. A woman's voice—piercing—piercing through the uproar and the din—not loud and yet cutting through it all like a sharp sword. Silence descends on us all except the singer—and her voice comes through piercing and sweet—filled with a fierce Gypsy emotion—lovely and rare version of *Barb'ra Allen*. There is the girl's voice—the crackling of the fire—otherwise complete silence. Not a tiny child murmurs. Little children, on their mothers' or aunties' laps, gaze with huge dark eyes that reflect the leaping flames of the fire. Mouths open—they gaze at the singer. Suddenly, with an almost un-bearable feeling of—almost vertigo—like a man coming out of chloroform—I am made aware that the moon is swinging up over the slag heaps, that there are stars above us—that a cool breeze is blowing—that the world, although it might be a dying planet, is unutterably beautiful.

The singer stops. There are tears on people's cheeks. These people are not listening to 'a folk song' in a drawing-room—they *believe* in Barb'ra Allen—they feel intense sympathy for young William. 'And from his heart grew a red red rose—and from her heart a briar!'

The silence—the almost unbearable emotional tension—is

broken by the loud hooting of an owl—and everybody howls with laughter!

'I'm fuckin' goin' to bed!' cries a young man.

'Yes—all you thinks about is *minj*!' shouts another.

'Gonna make them caravan springs creak and groan I reckon,' says a woman.

Somehow these people are alive! Their emotions are raw—unclothed—open to any stimulus. When I am with them I feel alive too.

'John—you sleep in my scrap van,' says Nelson. 'Got more room in there than that van of yours.'

I crawl in to the back of a closed scrap van—a shower of blankets is thrust in upon me.

Next day we are all fairly chastened. But a *yog* is lit, there is tea, bacon and fried bread. I have got to go—further into England.

At lunchtime I stop at a pub—one of those large, tarted-up pubs—garish wallpaper—mostly made to look like Cotswold stone or other folksy building materials, meretricious stamped brass objects, several pin-table machines.

The customers look like the inmates of the dyspepsia ward at a third-rate hospital. Ah, but it is a *respectable* pub. No 'Gypsies or Van Dwellers' would be allowed in here. Boredom has eaten into these people's souls like the maggot into a rotten apple.

I have trouble swallowing my beer. The fat landlady gives me a synthetic smile. 'Terrible weather, isn't it?' she says.

'Bugger the weather!' I am horrified to hear myself say, and I walk out into the rain.

It is difficult to run with the hare and hunt with the hounds though. When on my farm I am a farmer, and I mix with farmers, and, although I am always delighted when Travelling friends call, somehow I don't identify with them quite the same as I do when I am a Traveller myself. And I am glad I was born a *Gaujo*—a man of the settled race. Because, after all, we do grow the food, don't we, and till the land, and build the ships that sail the oceans, and—ah yes, we do a lot of terrible things too. It wasn't the *Gypsies* who made the atom bomb, or devised Belsen (they were inside it). I suppose every man (every *Gaujo* at least—maybe true Nomads are different) is a split man: one part of him wants to wander, the other to stay at home. I often envy such of my neighbours (and that is most of them) who are able to think: 'I was born here, my ancestors were born and buried here, and I will be buried here too'. George Hughes has often said to me: 'John—four generations of my forefathers were born and died in this house. And I will never leave it until I am carried out in a box—and you'll be carrying one corner of it!' Ah George—this is one service I would rather you did for me than I did for you!

But I have Gypsy friends about here too, and my left hand knoweth not what my right hand doeth.

Hangover

Help!
I've got the most villainous hangover today
I'm sure my efficiency's being undermined
It's no good asking me to make this rhyme
Or scan
Or do anything at all difficult
Do you mind?
I went to a pub called The Rampion last night
And came out rampin' drunk. I met friends in there
Romany *raklis* who *pukka* and *kushti jib*
And they put whisky in my *livena*
And when I drank it shouted for more
'How d'ye get on for *minj* these days?' asked Bish
'It's not *minj* I lack' I said 'it's *cor*.'
And we all spent a lot of wealth
And it's no good asking me what all these words mean
You'll have to find that out for yourself
We sang, lied, boasted, I kissed the landlady
And tried to get off with her granddaughter
In fact got her on my knee
But she *jelled* off with some horrible fellow
Young enough to be her brother—*ach y fi!*
'Go on—sing the Yellow Handkerchief!' shouted somebody
'Go on—give order please!'
'Give 'im order—order for Seymour!'
'Come on John—want me to go down on me knees.'

Oh order me no order I'm no better than I oughter
Be I sail towards Eternity another drink oh order me
But order me no order me but sing oh sing it had to be.
Oh fiddling and dancing were all my delight
And keeping flash company by day and by night
So keep the yellow handkercher in remembrance of me
And wear it round your neck while in flash company!
'Now Anna do a step! I'll tune for yer Anna while yer does a
    step!'
'Where's me harmonica!' And Anna did a step
And Nels stood up against her. Arms tight to side
Eyes staring straight ahead—immobile save their feet
They danced their intricate dance. Their faces ran with sweat
'Oh Gawd!' yells Nels. 'Oh *dordi*!'
'Go on!' we roared. 'You'll beat her yet!'
But Anna danced alone.
We clapped and stamped
And roared and ramped
And Anna danced—her dance a song—her dance a poem.
She danced alone.
We dance alone from the time we leave the womb
Even in lovelock until we reach the tomb

How I got home will probably never be revealed
I'll try to tell a little if time allows
I know at one juncture I found myself in a field
Preaching to a herd of cows
'Sisters!' I cried. And then I can't remember exactly what
    I said
Made them a speech. Preached them a sermon. No heresy
Nothing wrong
They gazed at me with their great soft eyes. Chewed their cud
And then I sang them a song
And then I thought I heard the nightingales
'But we don't have 'em!' I bellowed, scaring all the birds in
    the wood
'We don't have 'em in Wales
'Like they don't have robins in Spain
'Every man his own nightingale here'

But there they were—at it again
Trilling away like mad with jug jug jug
Oh the wonder of it! But suddenly I became aware that day
    was breaking
And then I felt a hell of a mug
For this was the dawn chorus I was hearing and every bird in
    the wood was trilling
Save nightingales. Just ordinary birds: thrushes and black-
    birds and Greater Spotted Fly
Catchers. Oh the glory of it! And I sat down on a rock and
    gave myself up to this song that seemed to fill the Earth
And bounce back from the sky!
And I was healed
And I climbed Carn Ingli
The little holy mountain near my home
My Hangover Mountain for I've nursed many a hangover up
    there
And gathered many a thorn too, and a bruise, and damn
    nearly risked my life
And when I got home breakfast was over
'Where the hell have you been?'
Said my wife

11 *Family Matters*

Furrowed is the brow of the man who is blessed with daughters, for you never know what is going to happen to them. Mine all took to horses at the appropriate points in their careers and I used to think, well, horses might break their necks but at least they will not put them in the family way. If you want to keep your daughter a virgin until she's out of the Fifth Form get her a horse. She will fall in love with that.

Clearly none of our daughters was bound for the cloister. That was evident. And I must say I quite *liked* the young men who came flocking round, with their beards and their guitars and their theories about this and that. I took against them at first of course—a father's natural jealousy—but then I found I liked them and they, after the first shock, found they liked our way of life at Fachongle Isaf, and our house was never without at least one young man serving his time, as it were, as a hewer of wood and a drawer of water and amusing us all by playing his guitar in the evening. And, by Jove, couldn't some of them play the guitar! We packed Jane off to America for a year once just to get her out of the melee. I have lots of cousins and uncles and aunts there and they were marvellous to her. When she came back I met her at the airport. After waiting an hour or two, mesmerized by the non-stop stream of humanity that issued from the pipe line, there was a temporary lull, or space, and I saw our Jane, wafting along like a piece of thistledown being blown along by a gentle zephyr, wearing a cookie broad-brimmed cowboy hat, shorts the brevity of which brought a blush even to my cheek, and carrying nothing but an enormous guitar. Where is her nightie and her toothbrush? I wondered. But that unspoken question was soon answered—after her staggered a Puerto Rican medical student pushing an enormous trolley loaded with heavy trunks. My daughter had come home.

Then the next thing was that she was going to get married. Not to the Puerto Rican but to a boy named Dave. A Wasp as the Americans say.

We were desperately short of buildings at Fachongle Isaf. We had no hay barn for example (the crazy erection that had been there when we arrived simply keeled over one day—a day of no wind and gentle rain. It simply, before our eyes, swayed over and collapsed to the ground, much as the Tower of Pisa is sure to do if it goes on leaning any further). Now my dear friend Bishop Burton, who owns a scrap yard near Cardigan, put me in the way of a large army hut, which lay in sections, in a great rotting heap with mushrooms growing from it, in a village not far away.

I looked at this heap of apparent rubbish, saw that most of the timber was sound, realized that as *firewood* at the going price it was cheap, and bought the whole lot for two hundred and fifty pounds. Derek and Ron, Bishop's sons, helped me over with it in their lorry. It took about seven heavy loads, and nearly broke the backs of the three of us because the sections, of double planking on heavy timber, were enormous and wet, and the toadstools weighed quite a lot, and it formed a huge pile in our field, where it slowly settled down to rot again.

Two young Australians came to our farm: Graham and Margaret. They lived, as so many young Australian couples seem to do in Britain, in a V.W. van. Sally always resisted people who wanted to come and live on our farm, but when she got to know them generally came to like them very well. This was the case with this couple, only more so than usual. Graham and Margaret spent a whole summer with us and we all got to love them, and they even got married from our house—at the almost impossibly picturesque little 'Church in Wales' (i.e. Anglican) church up in our valley, in which the Trefdraeth vicar holds a service once a month. The kids all got to work (there seemed to be a lot of them about just then), and decorated the church with all sorts of vegetation (I even saw some deadly nightshade around the pulpit but felt that this was no time for botanizing), and Graham and Margaret insisted on partly re-writing the marriage service to make it more acceptable to their liberal views, and Dave, Jane's new boyfriend, sat at the back and played a piece of music specially composed for the occasion on the guitar and, after the ceremony, we all went back to Fachongle Isaf and ate a sheep that had been roasted whole in front of the big fire. Everyone agreed that it was the most beautiful marriage that anybody had ever seen.

Well, what's all this got to do with the wooden hut? Only that, after the wedding, it suddenly occurred to me that there was this hut, and there were Graham and Margaret who both had the strength of ten, and Dave, and several others, and now would be the time to do something about it.

So we chose a site behind the Round Garden, which was a swamp and where nothing grew but flat irises, a site well hidden by the hill and by trees, and we dug down to hard ground, and built concrete pillars, and on these erected this enormous hut. And it *was* enormous, and in much better condition than we had thought it was going to be, with a double wooden roof, double walls, a fine wooden floor, marvellous strong well-made timber trusses, and only a few bits of rot here and there. We hove the enormously heavy sections into place, having to pull some of them up with block-and-tackle, and there was plenty of heaving, and shouting, and merry laughter, and amazingly nobody got flattened, and there stood this beautiful building. Well—beautiful? Beauty is in the eye of the beholder. In its army career it might have been a Naafi Hut, or a regimental orderly room with full suite of offices. At first I couldn't go into it without imagining a Regimental Sergeant Major marching an offender in in front of the Commanding Officer: 'Left right left right! Halt! Left Turn! Hat off! 6748593 Bombadier Smith. Sir!'

But gradually the kids got to work and demilitarized it. Away went the awful dark, murky, orderly-room green. Bright white paint covered everything. The window glass was replaced, an outer roof of some plastic stuff was nailed on top, doors were repaired, loving care was expended on that hut and it was made into a beautiful and human place.

But we didn't *really* know what to do with it. 'We'll call it the *Neuadd*,' I said. *Neuadd*, pronounced 'nayath', is Welsh for Great Hall: the place where people used to feast and make merry in days of old when this was a common activity.

Graham and Margaret went away to Australia. The big Hall stood there, quite empty, and I used to go into it, and stamp about on the great empty floor, and think what a magnificent building it was, and wonder what we should do with it. It was quite wrong for a hay barn. Too difficult to get to it, too difficult to get the hay in or out. But the more I looked at it, the more an idea began to take shape in my mind. A *Neuadd* it would be —a Great Hall in reality, where people could feel free, and welcome, and where true hospitality would be practised, and where the Spirit of Merry England would combine with Welsh *hwyl* (that untranslatable word) to produce a new synthesis: this wooden hut would become a Centre—a centre of a rural revival—a revival that would bring hard work, industry, fun and laughter, song and merry people back to this dying countryside.

I could stand on top of Parc y Banc (still can for that matter) and look about me at this beautiful valley, and, knowing what I know, see a picture of desolation. *That* farmhouse is a holiday cottage, occupied by foreigners a few months every year, *that* farm is a holiday cottage, in *that* one live retired, childless English people, in *that* one an old man, alone, *that* one, *that* one, and *that* one holiday cottages, in *that* an old couple, their children all gone to the cities, *that* one there, true, occupied by a striving young farmer, with a young family, trying hard to make a living, by more and more mechanization and chemicalization, in a hostile commercial climate—reminding me, as he gets deeper into debt in an effort to keep up with increasingly harsh conditions, of a dog chasing its own tail.

There are ruins all through our wooded valleys. There are more ruins than houses. Our little stone farmhouses, the huge rocks of which they are made held together with nothing but earth mortar, crumble away quickly when the roofs have gone. Two hundred years ago there was a big population here in this valley, and the land supported them. There were enough people here to sustain a high culture and civilization—an oral culture, true, but a culture of song, story, poetry, legend and history and an oral tradition going back to a time long before Hengist and Horsa landed on the coast of Kent. Where has it all gone? A few embers still glow—old men still sing songs and make poetry, or tell of brave days when twenty ór thirty farmers and their wives and children made up the shearing gang, and went round the valley from farm to farm shearing each member's sheep in turn, drinking home brew, feasting, and, after the hard work, singing and talking far into the night. The spirit—the tradition—still lingers on but there are no longer the *people* to sustain it.

Economic forces started the rot—landlordism in the seventeen and eighteen hundreds, when the Squire turned from being a benign leader of the community into a rack-renting landlord, then the lure of the coal mining valleys where all men could be free (what happened to *that* dream?)—these created the ruins. And now a set of misconceived planning laws keep them ruined. You cannot build a house in our area. You cannot rebuild a ruin. You cannot start a workshop to make a living. You cannot subdivide one of the big farms, so as to provide a living for more people. The agricultural advisers, who are living in the past, recommend that there should not be housing for more than *one worker per fifty acres* and the 'Planners', the great Nannies of our time, welcome this advice. A young man on a neighbouring farm to mine, from which the land had been sold off so that it only consists of buildings, went to Venice for three years to apprentice himself to a glass blower, came back and wanted to set up a studio in the disused cowshed. He intended to take on three young people from the village as assistants. No planning permission. The area was 'not scheduled for industrial development'. A man I know wanted to start a small factory in another disused cowshed for the manufacture of scientific instruments, at which he is a world expert. He would have employed six local young people. No planning permission. I wanted to build a house for another family on my farm. No planning permission. No, we must all just do as the authorities think we ought to do—fulfil their stereotyped idea of 'a farmer'. We must keep cows (oh yes—we are allowed to put up any amount of 'standard' agricultural buildings—prefabricated in huge factories away in England somewhere—as ugly as you like), put milk in bulk tanks, farm (or scratch-farm) with a minimum of labour (where is there for 'labour' to live?) with chemicals and machinery, and give up our fertile country to the *real*

purpose for which 'the Planners' think it fit: for it to be empty
scenery for the city person to gaze at through his windscreen
as he drives about the roads in his car. And the school-leavers
go on the dole as they leave school, and stand in little desolate
gangs on the street-corners of Newport.

I know a farmer who has the misfortune, like myself, to live
in a 'National Park' (a jobs-for-the-boys bonanza if ever there
was one!) and who was ordered to build his new cowshed of the
local stone (he should not have needed ordering). So he got to
work getting stone out of the little quarry by his house when an
'officer' drove up in a Landrover. 'Don't you know,' he said, 'no
quarrying is allowed in the National Park?'

'Where do you think *local stone* comes from?' asked my friend.
'Head office?'

There is a reverse current. People are coming out of the cities
again—coming back, after several generations, to claim their
birthright—a few acres of their own country. These people
know nothing about caring for the land, or growing food, or
looking after themselves in the country, *but they can learn.* Just
as their forefathers learnt to adapt themselves to city conditions
in the eighteenth and nineteenth centuries when they flooded
into the towns, so these people can learn about country conditions. They could take the half-deserted empty acres of
England, and of Wales and Scotland, and populate them again,
and farm them *intensively* to make them grow more food than
they ever grew before and, this is the important thing, with less
input. Gerald Leach, the Senior Fellow of the International
Institute for Environment and Development, has recently
written a book (*Energy and Food Production*—IPC) that the
average annual protein consumption of every person in Britain,
31 kilogrammes, now takes a quarter of a ton of oil equivalent
to produce it! His calculations show that in 1968 the UK food
supply system had an output of 261 megagigajoules and an
input of 1300 megagigajoules. Well, what on earth is the good
of this? What sort of 'efficient farming' is this? It would be more
'efficient' if we just drank the oil and had done with it. This
situation has arisen because of cheap oil and dear labour and
the lure of the towns. Oil is even now no longer so cheap in
relation to labour and in the future it will become less so. We

must get men and women back on the land! Only thus can we reduce our dependence on fuel and power.

And at present the men and women who are only too anxious to get back on the land are prevented by three things. One is they cannot get land, which is held in enormous units in this country by landlords who are hooked on high-power-input farming. The second is that they cannot get planning permission. (Here the remedy is easy—the present ridiculous and purely negative planning laws must be swept away. We must see that the energy which at present is devoted to stopping people doing things is diverted into making people do things.) The third is—ignorance. If they get their land—and their planning permission (or decide to do without the latter) they still don't know how to farm and don't know how to find out.

Well, I stood there, in my great empty *Neuadd*, and decided to do what one man may do to counter all this. I knew, and know now, it is impossible. How can one man—one man's will—fight a whole nation—a nation whom the gods, apparently wishing to destroy, make mad? But I have read my *Bhagavad Gita*, and anyway was familiar with what was in it before I read it, and I knew that it is not the achievement that is important, but the attempt; not the victory but the fight; not the goal but the journey. One must not even hope for, or think of, success, but concentrate all one's powers on the effort.

'This old army hut shall be a Centre!' I said. 'And I shall call it Canalfan Fyw, the Centre of Living. A movement shall start here that will radiate out over the countryside, and bring people back to the land, and fill the empty cottages, and rebuild the ruins, and the singing of men and women and the laughter of children shall once again ring through these woods and these fields shall become fruitful again!'

And to start off we'll have a wedding.

Jane and Dave Lewis had decided to get married. They were very prickly about it—no bride being given away by a doting Daddy, no this and no that, the Anglican ceremony being discreetly altered here and there to suit our susceptibilities, and the bridegroom to drive the bride, himself, up to the door of the church in a horse and cart. For we had a horse (not broken to the shafts it is true) and we had a cart: one that I had bought from the old butcher at Pont y Cwm many years before. It fell to Daddy of course to get the horse used to the cart, without smashing it—or him—to pieces but Daddies have their uses at times.

The great day approached. The little oh so beautiful deserted church in the valley was bedecked again with vegetation and flowers. No deadly nightshade this time, I was glad to see. The extremely nice and intelligent parson of Trefdraeth was very co-operative. On hearing that the bride and groom would be horse-drawn, people offered more carts and more horses. The owner of a riding stable at the Castle in Trefdraeth most kindly offered to lend us a dozen saddle horses. Work went on incessantly at finishing the decorating and the bedecking of the Great Hall. Beer was brewed in vast quantity, a turkey was killed, a ham got ready, huge displays of pies and pastries and puddings and Lord knows what were prepared: the distaff side of the community worked unceasingly in the steaming kitchen in preparation for the great day.

Which came.

We had tried to keep the wedding as secret as possible, but had, just quietly, dropped a word about here and there. Only relatives at the church of course. Our few nearest and dearest neighbours back at the farm, and close friends of the family.

The horses and horses and carts began to roll up. Lewis Cleverden, who had appointed himself Master of the Horse, and who wore a white flower in the hatband of his spectacular hat, shouted directions of which nobody took any notice at all. Everyone got mounted—the horses, unaccustomed to all this hullabaloo, restive. The cavalcade moved off. Sally and Dai and the parents of the groom went off on wheels, the bride and groom leading the way with Beauty pulling the butcher's cart (which had been gloriously painted for the occasion). We, of the boot and saddle, rode after—a gallant sight if ever there was one.

We were surprised to find that there were groups of people at every crossroad. It was as if they had turned out to see the Hunt. Thank God Beauty did not bolt. I knew it was quite on the cards that she might. But Dave, no more used to driving a horse than this horse was to being driven, coped well. When we got to the church the road was packed—there were fifty or sixty people there. There must have been a bad leak—somewhere.

Our arrival was heralded by Freddie Rees, the irrepressible auctioneer, blowing on a hunting horn. We pranced in among the crowd—which seemed to be swelling—got off our horses and handed them over to some good friends who had volunteered to hold them during the service.

In we went—to find just enough room in the front to sit down. The church was crowded with people. All went well, the service was very moving I thought, for our vicar is sincere and sounds it, and then I remembered I had got to read the Lesson. The passage about 'Faith, Hope and Charity, and the greatest of these is Charity.' I had been given the New English Version to read, didn't like it (how banal can writing get?) so had to go back to the St. James translation, didn't like the word 'Charity', so changed this to 'Love' which is what St. Paul really meant.

Vigorous beckonings from Mr. Griffiths informed me that it was my turn to go on. I staggered to the lectern, found that there was a Bible waiting there but that it was in Welsh, re-membered, thank God, that I still had the piece of crumpled paper in my pocket that I had scribbled the Epistle on, couldn't remember which pocket, was aware that my trousers were much too big and were slipping ever downwards, pulled them up again, couldn't find my reading glasses, and suddenly thought: 'If only I could play it for laughs!'

But finally I got myself together, read my bit, with sincerity because I believed in and liked what it said, and the situation was thus saved.

We rode away to another fine *tarrantalarrum* on Freddy's hunting horn, and back to the farm where champagne was brought out in a stirrup cup and drunk by all and sundry.

A hundred people crowded into the *Neuadd*. The place was packed but there would—and must—I realized, be always room for more. Freddie made a speech. Being an auctioneer he can get silence when he wants it and he did, and he was a fine sight in his morning suit with a carnation, his splendid spats, his marvellous growth of side whiskers, his noble moustache. He gave a most suitable speech and then he carved the turkey.

I stood beside him, feeling like the hero who stood on

Horatius' right hand and kept the bridge with him—and carved the ham. That ham and that turkey were like the widow's cruse —we went on carving them for ever and everybody had enough. And more than enough. Of course it was our own ham, our own turkey, properly reared and fattened according to well-tried methods on good well-grown food—not just incarcerated in some dark animal-factory, to be got ready for the supermarket.

The food was fine. The beer was fine. The champagne was— well, just champagne—but the discerning stuck to the beer. The music was fine. The groom, a fine guitarist and musician, had travelled with 'groups' and had good folk-singing and music-playing friends and we had there a magnificent folk band. Merriment knew no bounds. Some of us had decided to present the happy couple with a pig for a present, and this animal was introduced, when the revelling was at its height, into the *Neuadd*, with a blue and red riband tied round its neck. A young gilt, she joined eagerly in the proceedings. She dashed here and there, looking for scraps on the floor, knocked a few people over, there were screams, one felt that here was the time for a few ladies to faint. None obliged, though Menna Galli did run behind the animal with a dustpan and brush to clear up the somewhat copious droppings. I never saw a more contented pig.

The happy couple slipped away, as was expected of them (it would have looked a little bad if they hadn't), the parents (the other parents), departed, some of the older guests went, some of the younger just keeled over where they were. The band finally gave up through exhaustion, the singers because their throats were sore. By four in the morning there were scarce fifty of us left. And then that bleak time occurred when I discovered that the entire company—conscious, that is—consisted of Freddie Rees, Derek Burton—Bishop's son—and my good friend and companion Mrs. Elsie Band, the landlady of The Rampion Public House at Cilgerran, the best public house in the world. There we sat, like the shattered remnants of a victorious army resting in the midst of carnage, mopping up the last bottle of brandy that had been hidden as a reserve, but not hidden well enough.

'It's light!' I said. 'I must go to bed!'

'Go to *bed*?' said Fred. 'Why—the day's only just begun.'

139

It's no good asking me the way guvnor
I'm a stranger here myself
If you don't know the way I don't
And anyway the way to where?
Where is it you want to get to mate?
Someone said: 'I am the Way'
But he didn't make it clear where to
There's plenty of ways of course
This way and that way and the other way over there
They all lead somewhere—but is it anywhere you want to go?
Oh I'm a fool am I?
I see
Well I may be a fool master but I do know where I be
I live in a bubble of air I do
With a rock in it
Hurtling through Eternity
No it's no good asking me the way guvnor
I'm a stranger here myself
That's me.